CW01653200

IT'S SEW EASY

with JANOME

CREDITS

EDITOR Deborah Segaert
EDITORIAL ASSISTANT Fiona Murray
PROJECT COORDINATOR Irene Cowie
SUB EDITOR Margaret Kelly, Debra Banks
DESIGNER Jo Martin
PHOTOGRAPHY Joe Filshie
STYLING Georgie Dolling
PACKAGED BY Pride Publishing
PO Box 645, Rozelle NSW 2039
Tel: 61 2 9555 9322 Fax: 61 2 9555 6188
Email: info@pridepublishing.com.au

Prepress in USA, Printed in China by
Kaleido Graphics Services Group, Inc.

It's Sew Easy with Janome
ISBN 0957828977

pridepublishing

INTRO

The Janome Quilter's Companion series of sewing machines has been especially developed with the quilter in mind. With all the right stitches and features, these machines are the perfect choice – the perfect Quilter's Companion.

This book has been compiled by many talented and creative individuals to both inspire and delight you. Don't be put off by the title. If you're not a quilter, there are many projects here that use quilting techniques but have nothing to do with quilting! However, if you are a quilting enthusiast, within these pages you will find a plethora of ideas and projects to stimulate your imagination and creativity.

We have chosen home décor as the theme, because we all love to decorate our homes and make gifts that are both practical and beautiful. Home décor has become increasingly popular as we are exposed to new products, fabrics and design ideas featured on the many lifestyle television programs. All we need is inspiration and a little help from our friends.

The projects in this beautiful book have been carefully chosen to provide varying degrees of difficulty, enabling even the beginner to produce stunning and satisfying results. However, be warned, once you start on these wonderful ideas, you won't want to stop.

The projects have been constructed using the Quilter's Companion machine range. If you turn to page 64 you will see comparable stitches on the other models. Alternatively, choose your own decorative stitch substitutes. You do not need to be experienced in patchwork to undertake these projects. The methods are fairly general and you have probably used them or variations in some way in your sewing to date. There is however, one technique that you may not be familiar with – rotary, or speed, cutting. This technique is largely embraced by quilters as a preferred way of cutting fabrics for quilt making. You too can use it in these projects, whether they are patchwork or not. Wherever this method has been used you will see the instructions referring to cutting strips and shapes in the absence of templates. Turn to page 63 for detailed instructions on how to rotary cut your fabrics.

Please enjoy our book, enjoy your sewing and most importantly, enjoy your Janome Quilter's Companion.

CONTENTS

Bedroom

8 Flying Down the Borders Quilt
10 Valance
11 Curtains
12 Square Cushion
14 Round Cushion
16 Bolster Cushion

Sitting Room

36 Tablecloth and Skirt
39 Cushion
44 Lampshade
47 Freehand Embroidered Landscape
49 Footstool

Baby's Room

20 Irish Hearts Quilt
23 Wallhanging
24 Basket
26 Curtain Tie Backs
27 Butterfly
27 Towel and Washer
29 Bed Linen
32 Lacey Lucy

Outdoor Setting

52 Placemats
53 Serviettes and Serviette Rings
54 Director's Chairs
55 Chef's Hat, Apron and Oven Mitt
57 Cutlery Roll
59 Bread Roll Holder

60 Buying a New Machine
61 Quilting Attachment Set
61 Rotary Cutting
62 35th Anniversary
64 Quilter's Companion Models Stitch Comparison
65 Selecting the best needle for your project

BEDROOM

The bedroom is the place where you can combine your favourite colours and designs.

These projects include the traditional pieced patchwork pattern – flying geese.

This provides a strong design element and ensures the cushions and quilt complement each other. The flying geese units are simple to construct and the use of a 'strippy' quilt pattern means even a non-quilter can expect excellent results.

The quilt, cushions, valance and curtain border trims could be stitched on any of the Quilters Companion sewing machine series.

Flying Down

THE BORDERS QUILT

Coordinated fabrics make room planning an easy task, as this bedroom illustrates. The quilt was made with the traditional block, flying geese, and constructed using quick piecing techniques and a selection of print and border fabrics.

Requirements

- 50cm (20in) of six assorted print fabrics in dark, medium and light tones for geese
- 2.65m (2¾yds) of print fabric for geese and inside border
- 4.7m (5¼yds) of border print fabric for dividing strips and outside border
- 3.4m (3¾yds) of cream fabric for geese background and binding
- 2.7m x 240cm (3yds x 2½yds) wide fabric for backing
- 2.7m x 240cm (3yds x 2½yds) batting
- Neutral cotton thread for piecing
- Rotary cutter, mat and ruler

Janome Accessories

- Walking Foot – 214873013
- ¼in Seam Foot – 200008107

Cutting

From the length of the inside border fabric cut,
2, 1½in x 88in strips
2, 1½in x 66in strips

From the length of the outside border fabric cut,
2, 5¼in x 90in strips
2, 5¼in x 75½in strips
6, 5¼in x 88in strips for border print panels
All remaining strips are cut across the fabric width.

From the background fabric cut,
21, 3⅜in-wide strips. Crosscut into 245, 3⅜in squares. Cut these squares diagonally to make 490 half square triangles.
9, 2½in-wide strips for the binding.

Illustration 1

Illustration 2

From each of the seven assorted print fabrics cut,
9, 6¼in squares. Crosscut on the diagonal twice. This will create 36 triangles from each colour, of which 35 will be required. A total of 245 triangles of assorted prints are needed for the flying geese.

Piecing

Place the ¼in Seam Foot on the sewing machine. With right sides together, sew the light half square triangle to the side of the print triangle. Press the seam towards the light triangle, as shown in illustration 1.

Stitch another light half square triangle to the opposite side and press the seam toward the light fabric to complete the flying geese unit, as shown in illustration 2.

Sew a total of 245 flying geese units in the same manner.

To make a flying geese strip, sew together one each of the seven different fabric prints in order, referring to the photograph on page 9. Press all seams toward the printed triangles. Make 35 flying geese strips.

Sew together five flying geese strips to create one longer strip, making sure that the colour combinations of the flying geese are all in the same direction. Press. Make seven long flying geese strips.

Quilt Assembly

Join a flying geese strip (the flying geese are pointing down) to a border strip. Alternating the direction of the flying geese on the second strip, repeat the sequence with the remaining strips. Press all seams towards the border print.

Borders

Stitch the two, 1½in x 88in border strips to either side of the quilt and press the seams towards the borders. Sew the 1½in x 66in border strips to the top and bottom. Press seams towards the borders.

Repeat the process for the outside border.

Quilting

Layer the backing fabric, batting and quilt top, and baste or secure with safety pins.

Using the Walking Foot, ditch stitch down all vertical seams and around the borders.

Binding

Join the nine strips using a bias seam to make one long strip. Press in half wrong sides together. Sew binding to the right side of the quilt, mitring each corner. Trim around the quilt. Fold binding to the back of the quilt and slipstitch in place.

Valance

A valance covers the base of the bed down to the floor. There are two sections to a valance, the top that covers the base under the mattress, and the skirt. As all beds vary in size follow the instructions below to work out fabric requirements.

Requirements

- Determine measurements and purchase quantities of fabric to suit
- One of the print fabrics from the quilt for the skirt
- Calico for the base
- Crochet cotton

Method

For the valance with a gathered skirt, you will need between one-and-a-half to twice the measurement around the base, by the height of the bed, plus 5cm (2½in) for hem and seam allowance.

Select one of the print fabrics of the quilt to make the skirt.

As the base section is not seen, it can be made of inexpensive fabric such as calico.

Cut strips of print fabric for the skirt and join the strips to obtain the required length.

Sew a double 2.5cm (1in) hem on the lower edge of the skirt and at the skirt ends. Press.

Divide and mark the skirt into four equal portions. Select zig zag on the sewing machine and position the crochet cotton under the foot. (This is a quick easy way to achieve gathering.) Stitch over the crochet cotton, making sure it does not catch in the stitching.

Cut the calico to the size of the bed base, allowing for a 2.5cm (1in) hem at the top end and 12mm (⅝in) on the other three sides.

Sew a double 1cm (½in) hem at the top end. Press.

Divide and mark the base into four equal parts.

Pull the crochet cotton to gather the skirt, and with right sides together, match the skirt sections to the base marks.

Pin to distribute the gathers evenly, then sew the skirt and base together using a 15mm (5⅛in) seam allowance. Neaten the seam and press.

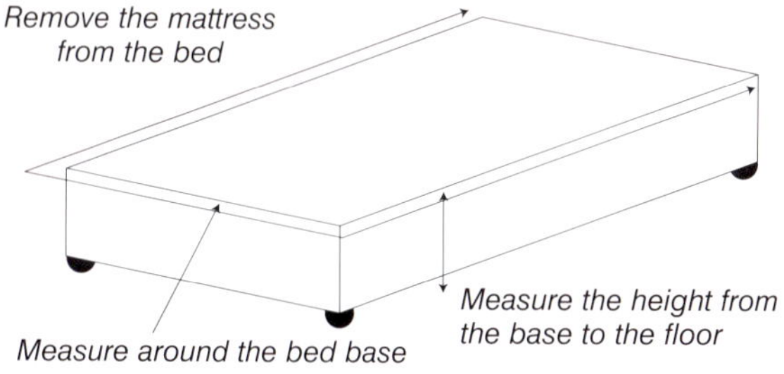

Curtains

Store-bought curtains can be decorated to match your bedroom's décor. The curtains in this bedroom have had strips of coordinating fabric stitched down both sides and large buttons have been covered with the same fabric and stitched across the curtain header.

Square CUSHION

The effects of ruching add nicely to this cushion. Simple piecing, couching and stitch building combine to make an attractive pattern.

Requirements

- 60cm (23 1/2in) light tone-on-tone fabric
- 15cm (6in) medium print fabric
- 20cm (8in) dark print fabric
- 40cm (16in) light floral print
- 50cm (20in) light-weight iron-on interfacing
- 45cm (15in) zipper
- Embroidery threads: dark, medium and light colours to match fabric
- Sewing thread for construction
- 2 skeins no. 5 crochet cotton (1 light, 1 medium)
- Tear-away stabiliser
- Quilter's imperial ruler, rotary cutter and mat
- Cushion insert (handmade or purchased)
- Twin needle size 2.5
- Triple needle size 3.0

Janome Accessories

- Janome blue-tipped needles – 990311000
- Bobbin Fill – J-208 or J-208-1
- 1/4in Seam Foot – 200008107
- Custom Crafted Foot F – 822804004
- Cording Foot H – 820819006

As this cushion has been constructed using an imperial quilter's rule, there is no direct conversion to metric. To recreate it accurately it should be constructed following the imperial measurements provided and rotary cutting methods. All seams are stitched using a 1/4in Seam Foot.

Decorative stitches use the Custom Crafted Foot F with tear-away stabiliser.

Cutting

From the light tone-on-tone fabric cut,
2, 21in x 1 1/2in strips
2, 14 1/2in x 1 1/2in strips
2, 20in x 12in pieces for cushion back

From medium print fabric cut,
2, 20in x 1 1/2in strips
2, 12in x 1 1/2in strips
4, 6 1/2in x 1 1/2in strips

From dark print fabric cut,
2, 38in x 3in strips for ruching
2, small triangles (using template on pattern sheet)

From floral print fabric cut,
1, 24 1/2in x 5 1/4in strip for the centre panel
2, 10in x 3 1/4in strips

Method

Cut both ends of the 24 1/2in x 5 1/4in strip of floral print fabric to a 45-degree arrowhead using the pattern on the pattern sheet as a guide.

Join the 20in x 1 1/2in medium fabric strips to either side of the floral centre.

Sew a 6 1/2in x 1 1/2in medium strip to either side of the floral centre ends, mitring the points.

Add the 21in x 1 1/2in light strips to either side of the centre piece.

To create the ruche panel, sew rows of gathering stitches 1cm (1/2in) apart, along the length of the two dark 38in x 3in strips.

Draw up the gathering threads evenly until the work measures 19in. Press the iron-on interfacing to the underside.

Attach the Cording Foot H and thread with light coloured embroidery thread. Select zig zag, width 1.5, length 1.0 and using the light crochet cotton, stitch three rows of stitching down the strip length in the centre slot, over the ruching in a gentle curving motion.

Change the sewing thread and the crochet cotton to the medium colour and stitch vertically across the light coloured cording.

Add the ruched strips to either side of the light fabric strips. Remove the gathering threads.

Continue to build the cushion front, adding the 14½in x 1½in light strips, the 12in x 1½in medium strips and the 10in x 3¼in floral strips. Lastly add the two small triangles.

Select stitch 36, width 3.0, length 1.0 and using light coloured embroidery thread, sew a line of stitching between the light cording on the ruched fabric strip.

Change to the triple needle and thread the machine with light, medium and dark embroidery threads. Select stitch 70, width 3.0, length 2.0 and sew down the centre of the light fabric strips.

Change to the twin needle and dark and medium threads. Select stitch 47, width 3.5, length 0.2 and sew the scallop stitch against the seam lines, with the curve of the scallop facing the triple needle stitching.

Use this stitch on the dark print in both corners, where the triangle joins the floral print.

Trim the cushion front.

To make the cushion back, use the two light fabric pieces, inserting the zipper into the centre back seam.

Trim the cushion back to match the size of the cushion front and with right sides together, stitch around the cushion edges. Leave the zipper open, so you can turn through the cushion to the right side.

Place a cushion insert inside the completed cushion.

Round
CUSHION

The centre of this cushion utilises stitch building and ribbon, whilst the outer panels are mainly flying geese units. Stitch building with ribbons enhances the sides.

Requirements

- 70cm (27½in) light tone-on-tone fabric
- 15cm (6in) medium print fabric
- 40cm (16in) plain dark fabric
- 30cm (12in) light floral print fabric
- 3.5m (3yds) of 3mm (⅛in) satin ribbon
- 3m (2⅞yds) of 5mm (¼in) piping cord
- 45cm (15in) zipper
- Embroidery threads: dark, medium and light colours to match fabric
- Sewing thread for construction
- Water-soluble marking pen
- 2B pencil
- Quilter's imperial ruler, rotary cutter and mat
- Tear-away stabiliser
- Cushion insert (handmade or purchased)

Janome Accessories

- Janome blue-tipped needles – 990311000
- Bobbin Fill – J-208 or J-208-1
- ¼in Seam Foot – 200008107
- Piping Foot – 200002101
- Custom Crafted Foot F – 822804004

As this cushion has been constructed using an imperial quilter's ruler there is no direct conversion to metric. To recreate it accurately it should be constructed following the imperial measurements provided and using rotary cutting methods. All seams are stitched using a ¼in Seam Foot.

Decorative stitches use the Custom Crafted Foot F with tear-away stabiliser.

Cutting

From the light tone-on-tone fabric cut,
2 half circles 18½in diameter, with 1½in added to the straight edge for the cushion backing
1, 5in x 44in strip for cushion edging
1, 5in x 13in strip for cushion edging
32, 2¼in squares for flying geese
1, 4¼in square for cushion centre

From medium print fabric cut,
8, 4in x 2¼in rectangles for flying geese
8, small triangles (using the template on the pattern sheet)

From dark print fabric cut,
1, 1⅜in square for cushion centre
8, 4in x 2¼in rectangles for flying geese

From plain dark fabric cut,
1¼in strips on the bias (joined for piping)

From floral print fabric cut,
3, 1¼in x 44in strips, then cross cut into 24, 5in lengths
2, 5½in x 1⅛in strips for cushion centre
4 pointed shapes (using the template on the pattern sheet)

Method

Centre Square

Onto the 4¼in square light tone-on-tone fabric, draw a cross dividing the square into four small equal squares, using the water-soluble marking pen. Refer to illustration 1 for stitch placement on the centre square.

Select stitch 65, width 7.0, length 2.5 and with medium thread on the machine, sew down either side of the drawn line, leaving a 3mm (⅛in) space between the rows of stitching.

Select stitch 71, width 5.5, length 2.5 and with dark thread on the machine, position the 3mm (⅛in) satin ribbon down the centre of the two previous rows of stitching and sew over the ribbon.

Take the two 5½in x 1⅛in floral strips and turn the edges under by 3mm (⅛in). Satin stitch the edges, width 2.0, length 0.3 with the dark embroidery thread, making sure the needle swings over the edge of the fabric.

Onto the centre square, pin these strips diagonally from corner to corner.

Place the $1^3/_8$in dark square onto the centre of the centre square, over the pinned diagonal strips. With the same machine settings, satin stitch the small square in place.

This square can now be trimmed to 4in.

Flying Geese

Draw a pencil line diagonally across the 32, $2^1/_4$in squares of light fabric. With right sides together, position a light square on the left corner of a 4in x $2^1/_4$in rectangle.

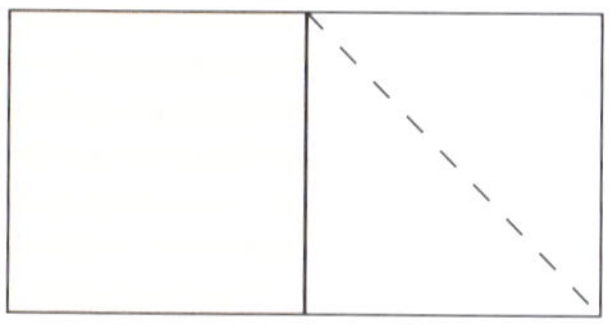

Diagram 1 – Stitch from corner to corner.

Stitch on the line, trim the seam to 7mm ($^1/_4$in) and press the seam to the light fabric (diagram 1). Repeat the process at the opposite corner of the rectangle. Make 15 more in the same manner. These are the flying geese units (diagram 2).

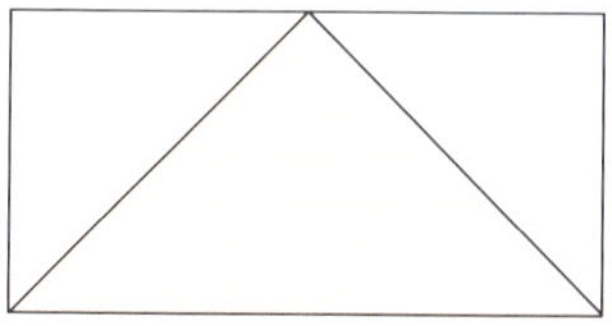

Diagram 2 – Flying geese unit

Select stitch 31, width 2.5, length 1.5 and using medium thread on the dark geese and dark thread on the medium geese, sew from the peak down, on either side of the triangle. This feather stitch should just meet the edge of the triangle.

Join four geese together, (medium, dark, medium, dark) to form four geese units. Take two of these units and stitch to either side of the centre square, with the base of the triangle aligned to the side of the centre square.

Sew a triangle to each side of the floral arrowhead shape to create one large triangle. Make four the same.

Stitch a geese unit between two large triangles. Make two the same. Sew one of these units to either side of the centre strip, taking care to match seams to the centre square.

Cushion Back

Make the cushion back from the light fabric with the two half circles. Insert the zipper, press, then trim the backing to the size of the cushion front.

Using the piping foot, make the piping with the bias strip and sew the piping to the edge of the top and bottom cushion pieces.

Illustration 1

Cushion Sides

Join the two 5in light fabric strips together along a short end. Measure the outside edge of the cushion top and seam the 5in strip in a circle to this measurement.

Commencing at the seam, divide the fabric into 24 equal parts, drawing a line at each point with the water-soluble marking pen.

Repeat the decorative stitching technique given for the centre square, sewing over the drawn lines. Using dark thread, add stitch 50, width 4.5, length 0.3 to both side edges of the decorative stitching.

On the three, 44in x $1^1/_4$in strips, turn under the raw edges 3mm ($^1/_8$in) and satin stitch, using the same instructions as those given for the centre square. From these three strips, cut 24, 5in lengths.

Gather the centre of each 5in length by hand and stitch in place between the rows of decorative stitching. Catch only the gathered centre to the centre of each space, using a needle and thread.

Select zig zag, width 7.0, length 0.2 and drop the feed dogs below the throat plate.

With dark thread on the machine, zig zag over the hand sewing, allowing the needle to swing to either sides of the strip 10 or 12 times.

Thread the machine with medium thread, select stitch 52, elongate x 2, width 7.0, length 0.2 and lock stitch to memory. On each side of the stitched gathers, sew a single pattern.

Straight stitch the top and bottom of the cushion side panel to attach the 5in strips before sewing the panel to the cushion top and bottom.

Either make or purchase a cushion insert and place into the completed cushion.

Bolster
CUSHION

Snuggle up with a comfy bolster that shows off your stitch building skills.

Requirements

- 50cm (20in) light tone-on-tone fabric
- 10cm (4in) medium print fabric
- 20cm (8in) dark print fabric
- 30cm (12in) light floral print fabric
- 20cm (8in) plain dark fabric
- 25cm (10in) heavyweight interfacing
- Embroidery threads: dark, medium and light to match fabric
- Sewing thread for cushion construction
- 45cm (15in) zipper
- Tear-away stabiliser
- Fusible webbing
- Water-soluble marker pen
- Twin needle size 3.0
- Quilter's ruler, rotary cutter and mat

Janome Accessories

- Janome blue-tipped needles – 990311000
- Bobbin Fill – J-208 or J-208-1
- Custom Crafted Foot F – 822804004
- 1/4in Seam Foot – 200008107

As this cushion has been constructed using an imperial quilter's rule there is no direct conversion to metric. To recreate it accurately it should be constructed following the imperial measurements provided and rotary cutting methods. All seams are stitched using a 1/4in Seam Foot.

Decorative stitches use the Custom Craft Foot F with tear-away stabiliser.

Cutting

From light fabric cut,
1, 23in x 6in strip for centre panel
2, 23in x 21/2in strips for outside edge
2, 221/4in x 31/2in strips for bolster ends

From medium print fabric cut,
12, 31/2in x 5/8in strips for bolster ends
6in square

From dark print fabric cut,
6in square
2, 22in x 2in strips for frills on bolster ends

From plain dark fabric cut,
6, 1in x 23in strips for flat piping

From floral print fabric cut,
2, 23in x 51/2in for centre panel strips
2, 2in diameter circles for bolster ends

From the fusible webbing cut,
2, 6in squares

Cushion tube

Using the 23in x 6in light fabric and a water-soluble marking pen, mark the fabric centre and draw a grid, 11/4in apart at a 45-degree angle across the fabric, making sure the first line crosses the centre point.

Repeat the grid in the opposite direction, again starting at the centre point (one of the rows of diamonds should be centred on the fabric).

With the twin needle and threads in a medium colour, select zig zag width 2.0, length 0.3 and sew over the drawn lines creating a double row of satin stitch.

Change to a blue-tipped needle, select stitch 51, elongate x 2, width 6.0, length 0.2 and lock stitch to memory.

Thread the machine with the darkest thread and starting from the centre, sew four individual patterns in a cross formation from alternative crossed lines.

To sew the flower centres, rethread with the lightest thread and alter the machine setting to width 7.0.

Select stitch 61, width 7.0, length 0.3, lock stitch to memory and sew a small heart over the alternative crossed lines.

Double all strips of dark fabric and press to form the flat piping.

With raw edges together, sandwich the flat piping between the embroidered panel and the floral strip. Sew together and repeat on the opposite side.

Divide each of the two 21/2in in light tone-on-tone fabric strips into 12 equal parts, drawing a line across the fabric at each of these points.

Press the 6in fusible webbing squares to the underside of the 6in medium and dark print squares and using the template from the pattern sheet, cut 12 half circles from each fabric.

Remove the paper backing from the fusible webbing and with raw edges together, alternate the fabrics, pressing the half circles over the marked lines.

Select zig zag, width 2.0, length 0.3 and satin stitch around the half circles, using a medium thread on the dark fabric and dark thread on the medium fabric.

Change to the twin needle and with medium coloured thread, sew a double row of stitching 22mm (7/8in) from the opposite edge using the same setting as the centre grid.

Return to the blue-tipped needle, select stitch 61, width 7.0, length 0.3, lock stitch to memory and with dark thread sew a row of small hearts under the double row of stitching and between the half circles.

Sandwich a piping strip as before, between the floral fabric and the half circle strips and sew. Add the last of the piping strips to the opposite sides.

Insert the zipper into the cushion panel.

The ends of the bolster are enhanced with decorative stitching.

Cushion Ends

Take one of the light coloured 22¼in strips and sew the ends together. Check that this piece measures the same as the cushion tube. Adjust if necessary and stitch the second strip to correspond.

Stitch placement

With the seam line as the first segment, divide these pieces into six equal portions, drawing lines with the water-soluble marking pen.

Press the fusible webbing onto the 12, 3½in x 5/8in strips and iron these over the drawn lines.

With dark thread on the machine, select zig zag, width 2.0, length 0.3 and satin stitch over the 12 strip edges.

Select stitch 47, width 5.5, length 0.3 and with medium coloured thread, sew a row of scallops down either side of the fabric strips, abutting the scallops to the satin stitch edge.

Sew a flower, 15mm (¾in) from the outer fabric edge, in the same manner as those stitched on the centre cushion panel.

On the edge opposite where the flowers are stitched, run two rows of gathering stitches and draw the threads tightly.

Baste the heavy interfacing to the 2in floral circles. Join a 22in x 2in dark print strip into a circle and fold wrong sides together, aligning the raw edges together.

Stitch two rows of gathers along the raw edge and draw in the gathering threads. Baste the 2in floral circle over the gathering to form a rosette. Make another the same.

With medium coloured thread, satin stitch, width 2, length 0.3, around the floral circles.

Join the end pieces to either end of the cushion tube.

Either make or purchase a cushion insert and place into the completed cushion cover.

BABY'S ROOM

The excitement and anticipation of a new arrival is an ideal time to sharpen your sewing skills and decorate baby's room.

The following projects use the Sunshine Acres range by RJR Fabrics. A similar coordinated range would also give the same beautiful results.

Making practical coordinated accessories means baby's room is also functional – linen and towels provide an opportunity for decorative stitches too. Stitching the freehand butterflies is a perfect small project to master the art of freehand embroidery.

Irish Hearts
QUILT

This beautiful quilt is a variation of the traditional Double Irish Chain quilt pattern. The Irish Chain consists of two alternating blocks and a pretty heart appliqué has been added.

Requirements

- 2.5m (2 3/4yds) aqua fabric for background and second border
- 1m (1yd) lilac fabric
- 75cm (30in) floral check fabric
- 2.8m (3yds) coordinating fabric for first border, binding and backing
- 1.2m x 2.4m (1 3/8yds x 2 3/4yds) batting
- Rotary cutter, mat and ruler
- 50cm (20in) fusible webbing
- Coordinating embroidery thread for appliqué
- Sewing thread for construction
- Template plastic
- Water-soluble marking pen
- Scissors

Janome Accessories

- 1/4in Seam Foot – 200008107
- Custom Crafted Foot F – 822804004
- Walking Foot – 214873013

Cutting

From the aqua fabric cut,
4, 5cm x 112cm (2in x 44in) strips
5, 15cm x 112cm (6in x 44in) strips
From these strips, cut 15, 15cm x 15cm (6in x 6in) squares and 30, 15cm x 5cm (6in x 2in) rectangles. The remaining strips will be used in the strip piecing.

From the lilac fabric cut,
16, 5cm x 112cm (2in x 44in) strips

From the floral check fabric cut,
8, 5cm x 112cm (2in x 44in) strips

Block A

Rows 1 and 5: Referring to the illustrations on page 22, join fabric strips making two strip sets.

Press all seams in the one direction then crosscut the strips at 5cm (2in) intervals. Thirty sets are required.

Rows 2 and 4: In a like manner, join the fabric strips following illustration 2, again making two strip sets. Press, then crosscut at 5cm (2in) intervals. Thirty sets are required.

Row 3: Stitch one strip set shown in the illustrations on page 22, pressing then crosscutting as before. Fifteen sets are required.

To piece Block A, refer to illustration, sewing the five strip sets together. Alternate the seam directions so that each strip 'locks' at the seam intersection. Make 15.

Block B

Rows 1 and 3: Stitch a 5cm (2in) lilac strip to either side of a 15cm (6in) aqua strip. Repeat with the remaining strips.

Press the seams in one direction and crosscut the strips at 5cm (2in) intervals. Thirty sets are required.

Row 2: Sew a 15cm x 5cm (6in x 2in) rectangle to either side of a 15cm (6in) square. Make 15 sets.

On either side of row 2, stitch rows 1 and 3, referring to block B illustration on page 22. Fifteen blocks are required.

Referring to the quilt photograph, alternate blocks A and B in horizontal rows. Assemble the blocks in rows, then stitch the six rows together. Press the seams towards block B.

Heart Applique

From the lilac fabric cut,
2, 5cm x 112cm (2in x 44in) strips
1, 2.5cm x 112cm (1in x 44in) strip
From the floral check fabric cut,
2, 5cm x 112cm (2in x 44in) strips
1, 2.5cm x 112cm (1in x 44in) strip

Make two strip sets, sewing a lilac and check floral strip together. Press seams to one side, then crosscut the strips at 5cm (2in) intervals. Thirty sets are required.

Make a four patch by stitching two sets together – with squares diagonally placed, alternating the seam direction so that the centre seam intersection matches. Press.

Referring to the illustration on page 22, with the four patch on point, angle the 2.5cm (1in) strips across the top two edges of the four patch. Create nine blocks with the lilac square top and bottom for the quilt rows 1, 3 and 5 and six blocks with the

Row 1 and 5

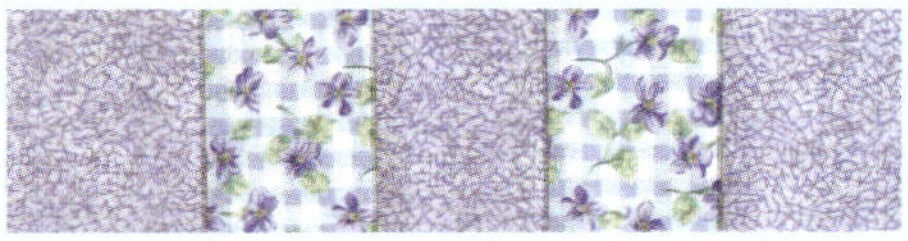

Rows 2 and 4

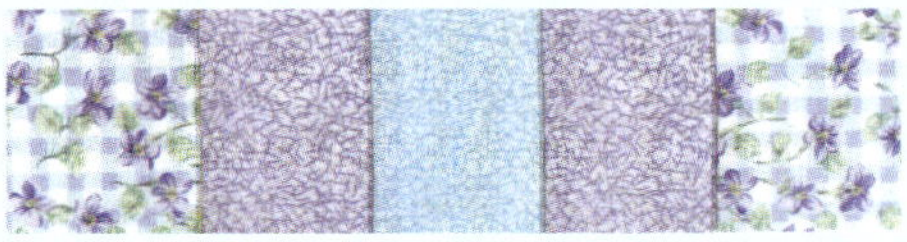

Row 3

Block A

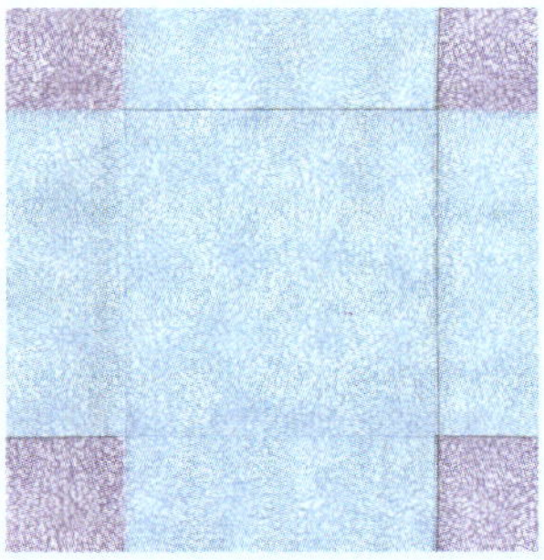

Block B

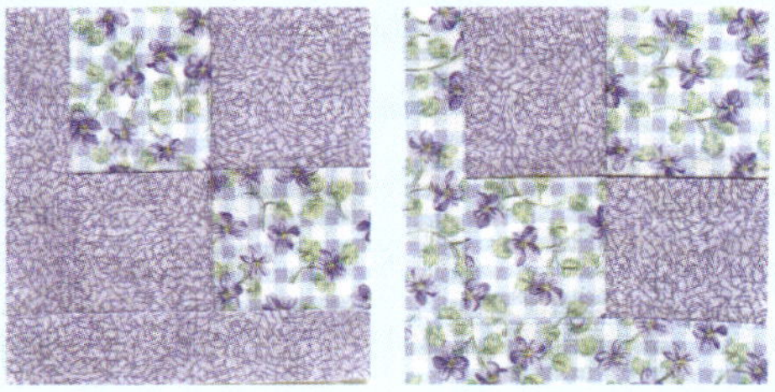

Create nine blocks with the lilac square at the top and six blocks with the floral check square at the top.

floral check square top and bottom for the rows 2, 4 and 6, coordinating the 2.5cm (1in) strips to match the top squares.

From the pattern sheet, trace the heart onto template plastic and cut out. Place the heart template onto the four patch block with the heart point aligning with the right angle of the bottom fabric square. Using the water-soluble marking pen trace around the heart. Cut out the fabric heart on the traced line. Repeat, creating 15 hearts.

Use the template again to trace and cut 15 fusible webbing hearts. With a pressing cloth, iron the fusible webbing hearts to the reverse side of the fabric hearts.

Remove the paper backing from the hearts and referring to the photograph for placement, press the appropriate heart to the centre of the B blocks.

Select stitch 26, and change to the Custom Crafted Foot F. Appliqué around all 15 hearts, using embroidery thread.

Borders, Binding and Backing

Halve the fabric for the borders, binding and backing, making two 140cm (55in) lengths.

Cut a 17.5cm (7in) strip from one of these lengths and join to the other piece to create the backing piece. Press the seam open and set aside.

From the fabric that had the 17.5cm (7in) strip removed, cut

4, 3.5cm x 140cm (1¼in x 55in) strips for the first border.

4, 6cm x 140cm (2½in x 55in) strips for the binding. Join these lengths on a 45-degree angle to create one length. Press the seams open and set aside.

From the aqua fabric cut,

4, 10cm (3¾in) wide strips by the fabric length for the second borders.

Measure the quilt length down the centre of the quilt and trim two of the first borders to suit. Stitch in place then iron, pressing the seams toward the border.

Repeat this process for the side borders.

Measuring the quilt length and width in the same manner, trim and sew the second borders in place. Press the seams towards the second borders.

Finishing

Layer together quilt backing, batting and quilt top. Pin or baste the layers together. Commence at centre and work outwards. With the Walking Foot attached, this quilt has been quilted in the ditch horizontally and vertically and across the diagonals of the pattern. After quilting is complete, remove basting and square-up top, batting and backing using rotary cutter, mat and ruler.

Fold the binding strip in half wrong sides together and press. Using the Walking Foot, stitch raw edges of binding to quilt edge starting halfway along one side, mitring all corners. Turn binding to the wrong side and hand stitch in place.

Irish Heart
WALLHANGING

Requirement

- Leftover fabrics from quilt
- Matching sewing thread for construction
- Coordinating embroidery thread for appliqué
- Fusible webbing
- Template plastic
- Water-soluble marking pen
- Scissors
- Rotary cutter, mat and ruler
- Decorative hanger

Janome Accessories

- Custom Crafted Foot F – 822804004
- Walking Foot – 214873013
- Darning Foot – 822820006
- 1/4in Seam Foot – 200008107

Cutting

From the aqua fabric,
Cut three, 15cm x 15cm (6 1/4in x 6 1/4in) squares

From the lilac fabric,
Cut four 15cm x 3cm (6 1/4in x 1 1/4in) strips
Cut two 57cm x 3cm (23 3/4in x 1 1/4in) strips

From the floral check fabric,
Cut two 21cm x 5cm (8 3/4in x 1 3/4in) strips
Cut two 67cm x 5cm (27 1/4in x1 3/4in) strips

Method

Referring to the photograph, stitch a 15cm (6 1/4in) lilac strip to the top and bottom of the centre square. Join the first and third square to the centre, adding a lilac strip at both ends.

Attach a long lilac strip to either side. Attach a 21cm x 5cm (8 3/4in x 1 3/4in) floral check strip to the top and bottom. Then, stitch the two remaining long floral check strips to either side.

Heart Applique

Referring to the heart appliqué instructions on page 20, make three four-patches from 6.5cm (2 1/2in) strips in readiness to cut heart shapes from.

Trace the wallhanging heart template from the pattern sheet onto template plastic and cut out. Cut out hearts and appliqué to the wallhanging in the same manner as used for the quilt.

Cut batting and backing fabric to fit the pieced front. Layer these three pieces together. Pin or baste the layers, commencing at the centre and working towards the outside edges.

Using the Walking Foot, quilt in the ditch using a straight stitch. Change to the Darning Foot, lower the feed dogs and stipple quilt the aqua squares.

Remove the basting, trim the excess backing and batting ensuring the wallhanging is squared-up.

Cut 6.5cm (2 1/2in) strips for the binding from the lilac fabric, join on the diagonal and press the seams open. Fold the strip in half wrong sides in and press. Pin the binding in place to the front of the wallhanging, aligning the raw edges of the binding to the raw edges of the wallhanging and sew, using a 7mm (1/4in) seam allowance. Turn the folded edge to the back of the wall hanging and slip stitch in place by hand.

Handstitch a small fabric strip to the back top edge of the wallhanging as a pocket to accommodate the dowel or rod of the decorative hanger.

Basket

Requirements

- Basket
- Batting to fit basket base
- Fabric to fit lining of base
- 30cm (12in) of three coordinating fabrics for base
- 40cm (15in) of fabric for side and overhang of basket
- Decorative thread
- Bias tape
- Elastic
- Tear-away stabiliser
- Rotary cutter, mat and ruler

Janome Accessories

- Bobbin Fill – J-208 or J-208-1
- Walking Foot – 214873013
- 1/4in Seam Foot – 200008107

Base

Measure the base of the basket and cut the lining and batting 2cm (1in) larger than the basket base. This will be trimmed to the correct size later.

Cut strips from the three coordinating fabrics at several different widths – 3.8cm (1½in), 6.3cm (2½in) and 9cm (3½in).

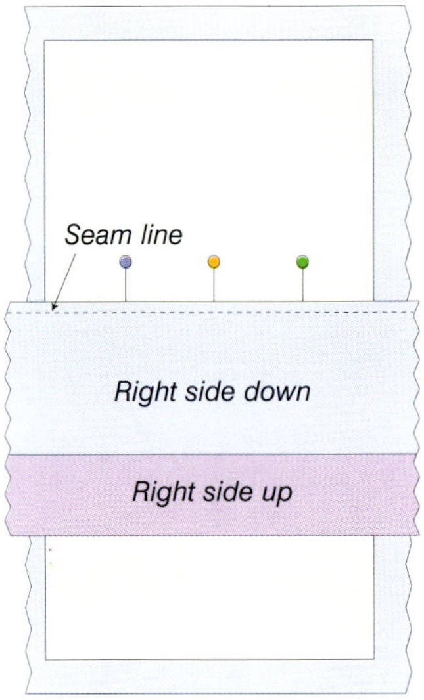

Diagram 1

Attach the 1/4in Seam Foot. Place the batting onto the wrong side of the base fabric. Position one of the strips, right side up, in the centre of the batting. Position the next strip, right side edges together, right side down and stitch, as shown in diagram 1.

Position the first strip right side up, then the second right side down and stitch in place along the right-side edge.

Fold back the second fabric strip to the right side and stitch a third strip to the second strip. Continue stitching the strips in place across the base towards the right edge. Spin the batting and base fabric 180-degrees and stitch strips in place working towards the other side.

Cut this continuous quilting to the basket base size, allowing a 1cm (½in) seam allowance.

Sides

Cut fabric strips to measure one-and-a-half times the outside measurement of the basket and a width of twice the depth.

Change to a normal presser foot and join the fabric pieces into a circle. Neaten the outside raw edge by turning a 1cm (½in) hem and straight stitch.

Using tear-away stabiliser to stabilise the work, use a decorative stitch to cover the straight stitch.

Position and stitch the bias tape for the elastic, approximately 5cm (2in) from the embroidered edge.

Sew two rows of long straight stitching near the raw edge and gather the fabric to the base dimensions.

Pin, then sew the gathered fabric piece to the quilted base, rounding the corners slightly to make attaching the frill easier. Neaten the raw edges. Insert the elastic into the bias tape.

Bows

Cut two, 75cm x 7cm (30in x 2¾in) strips from the main fabric and cut two, 75cm x 4cm (30in x 1¾in) strips from a contrasting fabric.

Place the fabric right sides together and sew down both long sides to form a tube, ensuring an opening for turning is left toward the centre. Centre the narrower fabric and press. Sew a V shape at either end and clip into the corner of the V, turn to the right side and press. Hand stitch the opening closed.

Tie the completed length into a bow and attach at either end of the basket by hand.

Curtain
TIE BACKS

Requirements

- 60cm (23²/₃in) fabric
- 3, 4cm x 115cm (1³/₄in x 45in) strips of contrasting fabric
- 60cm x 90cm (23²/₃in x 35in) iron-on Pellon
- 3.5m (3⁷/₈yds) of 5mm (2in) wide piping cord
- Matching sewing thread
- Water-soluble marking pen
- 2 large press studs
- 2 small rings
- 2 small screw-in hooks
- Quilter's ruler

Janome Accessories

- Walking Foot – 214873013
- Piping Foot – 200002101

Method

Create a template for the tie backs from the pattern on the pattern sheet. Cut four fabric and four Pellon tie backs using the template.

Iron the Pellon to the back of each fabric piece making sure the Pellon glue does not come into contact with the iron.

Onto a fabric piece, mark the centre and using the water-soluble marking pen and quilter's ruler, mark a 45-degree line across the fabric. Continue ruling a grid across the tie back at 2cm (1in) intervals.

Repeat this procedure on a second tie back angling the 45-degrees in the opposite direction.

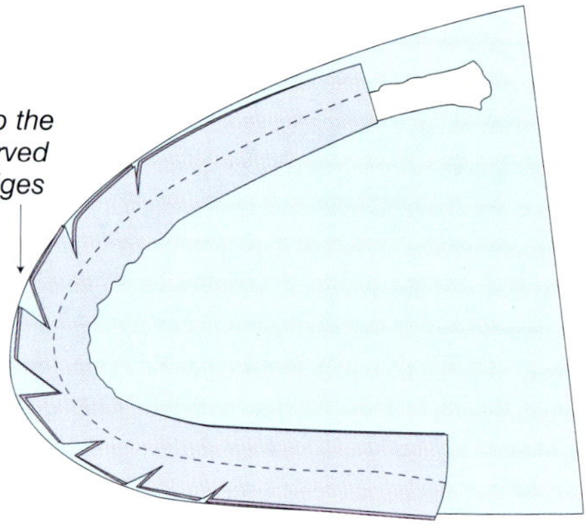

Diagram 1

Place the Walking Foot on the machine, select stitch 30, and using normal sewing thread, stitch on the marked lines.

The two remaining pieces are the reverse side of the tie backs and do not need to be as densely quilted. Therefore, rule lines across the tie back length at 5cm (2in) intervals and stitch in the same manner.

Join the three, 4cm (1³/₄in) wide strips together with a bias seam, using a 7mm (¹/₄in) seam, then press the seam open.

Change to the Piping Foot. Make the piping, referring to the manufacturer's instructions included in the packaging for the piping foot.

Commencing at the back top, stitch the piping to the right side of the tie back front, clipping the piping edge on the curved ends as shown in diagram 1.

With right sides facing, pin, then stitch the front and back pieces together leaving an 8cm (3¹/₈in) opening.

Clip where necessary, then turn the tie back through the 8cm (3¹/₈in) opening to be right side out. Hand stitch the opening closed, eliminate the water-soluble marking lines and allow to dry. Press.

Sew a press stud to the inside ends of both tie backs and a ring to the underside. (This ring will attach to a hook fastened to the window frame.)

Attach a freehand butterfly to a tie back if desired.

Butterfly

Requirements

- 20cm (8in) printed fabric to match the décor
- Fusible webbing
- Water-soluble stabiliser
- Embroidery hoop (inner hoop bound with cotton tape)
- Coordinating embroidery threads
- Water-soluble marking pen
- Tracing paper
- Bobbins filled with coordinated thread

Janome Accessories

- Darning Foot – 822820006

Method

Because both sides of the butterflies will be visible, the bobbin thread must coordinate with the upper thread.

Trace the butterfly from the pattern sheet onto the tracing paper, transferring all markings.

Press the fusible webbing to the back of the fabric and pin the traced butterfly to the fabric. Cut two pattern shapes for each butterfly from the fusible webbing-backed fabric.

Remove the paper backing from the fusible webbing and using a pressing cloth both under and over the fabric, press the set of wings together to form one butterfly. The edges may need to be trimmed if the two pieces do not match exactly.

Transfer all butterfly markings onto the fabric using the water-soluble pen.

Place the water-soluble stabiliser into the embroidery hoop and pin the fabric butterfly to the centre. Using a small zig zag, stitch around the shape to secure the butterfly to the stabiliser.

Drop the feed dogs and place the Darning Foot on the machine. Both upper and lower threads must be the same colour.

With the zig zag width set between 2 and 3, freehand (refer to page 48 for freehand embroidery technique) around the outside edge, moving the hoop both vertically and horizontally, allowing the stitches to drop over the edge.

Changing upper thread and bobbin each time, continue with a second, third, then fourth colour, combining and intermingling colours as desired.

Freehand the butterfly centre, changing colours to harmonise with the stitched edges.

Set the machine on a straight stitch to freehand the circles on the butterfly wings and to add definition to the centre.

Cut away excess stabiliser and rinse the stitched butterfly in hot water to remove any remaining stabiliser. Allow to dry, then press.

To create the butterfly body, make a roulette and cut into 7.5cm (3in) pieces. Knot one end of the roulette piece to make the butterfly head and neaten the other end. Secure the body to the centre of the wings with a straight stitch.

Make the feelers by stitching over three strands of thread with a zig zag stitch set at width 3. Knot the feeler ends and stitch to the butterfly body with a small zig zag.

Towel AND Washer

Requirements

For one towel and face washer:

- 1 strip x 115cm (42in) patchwork fabric (cut the width of the woven band on the towel and face washer plus 1cm (1/2in)
- 2.4m (2 3/4yds) of 10mm (1/2in) wide cotton lace
- Coordinating sewing thread
- Pins
- Embroidery thread
- Tear-away stabiliser

Janome Accessories

- Custom Crafted Foot F – 822804004

Method

Turn and press a 7mm (1/4in) hem on either side of the fabric strip.

Using Foot A, a straight stitch and normal sewing thread, stitch the lace to either side of the strip. Pin the border to the towel's woven band, folding under a small hem at the towel edges.

Change to the Custom Crafted Foot F and rethread with embroidery thread.

Select stitch 50, adjust the width to 4mm and the length to 0.3mm.

Place the tear-away stabiliser under the towel and sew a line of triangles directing the triangle peak to the edge of the fabric, as shown in illustration on page 27.

Repeat these steps to decorate a complementary face washer to add to your baby's room.

Stitch the triangles along the edge facing the lace.

Bed Linen

Cot mattresses and pillows can vary enormously in size, so it will be necessary to measure each piece of the cot linen to suit your needs.
The fabric quantity is based on cotton sheeting 242cm (95in) wide. Extra pillowcases and bassinet sheets can be created from the remaining sheeting.
Experiment with the decorative stitches on your machine to produce alternative bed linen trims.

Requirements

- 3m (3¼yds) of 242cm (95in) wide sheeting fabric
- 2m (2¼yds) of 2cm (1in) wide cotton lace
- White sewing thread
- Water-soluble marking pen
- Tear-away stabiliser
- 10cm (4in) coordinated patchwork fabric
- Ruler
- Seam ripper
- Embroidery threads

Janome Accessories

- Custom Crafted Foot F – 822804004
- Walking Foot – 214873013
- ¼in Seam Foot – 200008107

Pillowcase

The pillowcase is made from one length of fabric which has had a decorative trim added.

Measure the length of the pillow and add 18cm (7in) to allow for ease, the hem and the pillow flap plus the seam allowance for the decorative trim.

Measure the pillow width and add 3.5cm (1½in) to allow for ease and seam allowances.

Now, cut a piece of sheeting fabric to this calculated size.

For the decorative trim, cut a piece of fabric to the width of the pillow plus 3.5cm (1½in) by 13cm (5in) in length.

With the water-soluble marking pen and ruler, draw a line 3.5cm (1½in) from the bottom edge of this trim strip and mark the buttonhole positions using the guide on the pattern sheet.

Place the buttonhole foot on the machine and select buttonhole stitch, width 4, length 3. Position a piece of tear-away stabiliser under the fabric and sew the buttonholes on the marked positions.

Remove the stabiliser, erase the pen marks with water and allow the fabric to dry. Using a seam ripper, slit all buttonholes.

Detail of the decorated trim

Place the Custom Crafted Foot F onto the machine, select stitch 47, width 6, length 3. Rethread the machine with a coordinating embroidery thread.

With tear-away stabiliser under the fabric, sew a row of the scallop stitch either side of the buttonhole ends, butting the left edge of the Custom Crafted Foot F against the buttonhole bar tack.

Change to the 1/4in Seam Foot and normal straight stitch.

From the 10cm (4in) strip of patchwork fabric, cut two 4.5cm (1 3/4in) wide strips, join on the bias and press the seam open. Fold the fabric in half, right sides together and sew a 7mm (1/4in) seam along the raw edges of the length of the strip.

Turn the fabric through to the right side and press. This strip will be inserted through the buttonholes. There will be enough of the insertion left to use on the decorative trim for the top sheet.

After threading, secure each end of the trim with a straight stitch.

Change back to the Custom Crafted Foot F and rethread the machine with an embroidery thread.

Select stitch 80, and sew one flower between each insertion.

Rethread with a green embroidery thread, select stitch 51, width 4, length .3. Sew one leaf on either side of the previously stitched flower.

Return to normal sewing thread and presser foot. Trim the lower edge of the border strip 1.5cm (3/4in) beneath the lowest drop of the scallop stitch. In the same manner trim the top edge 4.5cm (1 3/4in) from the scallops' lowest edge.

With right sides together, sew the lace to the lower edge. Press the raw edges to the underside, exposing the lace.

Stitch the completed trim to the top of the pillowcase fabric with wrong sides together lining up the outside edge of the normal presser foot to the raw edges.

Press the decorative trim to the right side of the pillowcase fabric, then stitch down the trim as close to the lace as possible.

At the other end of the pillowcase, turn and press a 5mm hem. Turn the fabric a second time creating a 1.5cm (3/4in) hem and stitch with a straight stitch.

With right sides together, fold back the bordered side, the pillow length plus 3cm (1 1/4in). Press the fold.

Turn back the remaining fabric over the border edge and pin. Make sure both sides of this flap measure the same distance.

Straight stitch along both long sides through all thicknesses. Neaten the raw edges using an overlock stitch. Turn the pillowcase to the right side and press.

Top Sheet

Cut the sheet to the required mattress size allowing a generous tuck under.

To make the decorative trim, cut a 13cm (5in) strip the width of the sheet and follow the instructions given for the pillowcase.

On three sides of the sheet, fold and press a 7mm (1/4in) hem. Turn the fabric a second time creating 1.5cm (1 3/4in) hems. Straight stitch and press.

Fitted Cot Sheet

Because cots and mattresses vary in width, length and depth it is necessary to refer to the diagram below to calculate the dimensions to suit your mattress.

Cut a piece of the sheeting fabric to the following size:

Width: mattress width plus 2cm (1in) for seam allowances, plus twice the mattress depth plus 20cm (7in) for tuck under and seam allowances.

Length: mattress length plus 2cm (1in) for seam allowances and twice the mattress depth plus 20cm (7in) for tuck under and seam allowances.

From this piece, cut a square from each corner [mattress depth plus 10cm (4in)].

Each corner seam should be stitched with a French seam for neatness and durability. Refer to the diagram below to stitch the corner seams. With wrong sides together, join and pin the two A points and stitch to point B using a 4mm (1/8in) seam. Repeat on all four corners.

Turn the fabric to the other side and press the seam closed along the seam line. With right sides together stitch a 7mm (1/4in) seam, using the 1/4in Seam Foot.

Change to the normal presser foot, select Tricot stitch and adjust stitch to width 5 and length 2. Using fitted-sheet elastic, insert the sheet edge between the folded elastic and, stretching as you sew, stitch on the elastic around the edges.

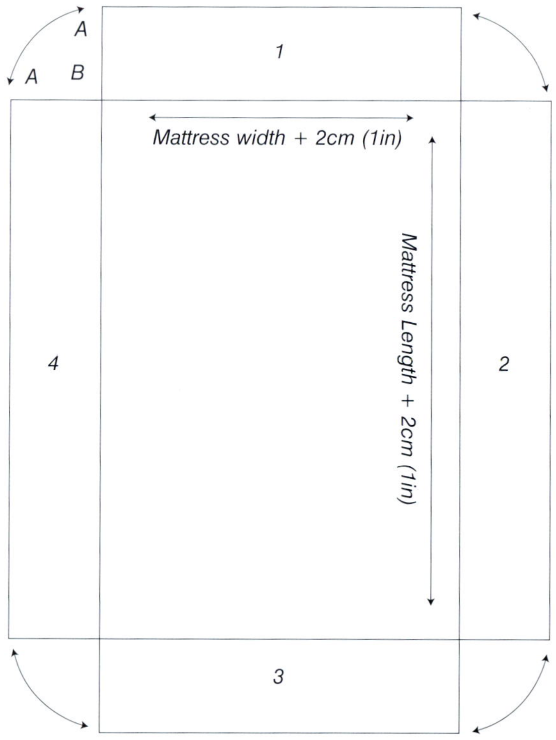

1, 2, 3 and 4 = mattress depth + 2cm (1in) + 20cm (7in) for tuck under and seam allowances.

Lacey
LUCY

Create this cute doll measuring 40cm ($15^{1}/_{2}$in). It makes the perfect decorative feature for any room or treasured friend for a child.

Requirements

- 30cm ($11^{7}/_{8}$in) diameter crocheted doily for doll top
- 30cm ($11^{7}/_{8}$in) homespun for body
- 25cm x 60cm ($9^{7}/_{8}$in x $23^{2}/_{3}$in) striped fabric for underskirt
- 23cm x 60cm ($9^{1}/_{8}$in x $23^{2}/_{3}$in) patterned fabric for outerskirt
- Template plastic or tracing paper
- HB lead pencil
- Polyester fiberfill for stuffing
- 1 reel of thread to match the homespun
- 1 reel of thread to match the yarn
- Crochet cotton
- 1m x 3mm (1yd x $^{1}/_{8}$in) ribbon (cut into four equal lengths)
- Tear-away stabiliser
- Embroidery threads
- Fine point permanent fabric marker
- Scissors
- 1 decorative button
- 13cm x 8cm ($5^{1}/_{8}$in x $3^{2}/_{5}$in) piece of cardboard
- Craft glue
- Yarn for hair
- Hand sewing needle

Janome Accessories

- $^{1}/_{4}$in Seam Foot – 200008107

Preparation

Trace all pattern pieces from the pattern sheet onto either template plastic or tracing paper. The outlines of the pattern pieces are the stitching lines.

Fold the homespun, right sides together and press. Place the templates on the fabric and trace around them with an HB lead pencil. Leaving 2cm ($^{3}/_{4}$in) between each pattern piece for seam allowances, trace one body and two arms.

Construction

Leaving the lower edge open (marked on the pattern sheet), use a straight stitch, length 1.5, to sew along the drawn pencil lines of the doll's body, back stitching at the beginning and end. Use the needle down position for ease when pivoting.

Cut out the pieces leaving a 7mm ($^{1}/_{4}$in) seam allowance all around. Clip the inside curves, then turn to the right side.

To create the legs, cut one, 15cm x 15cm (6in x 6in) piece of leftover skirt fabric and two, 15cm x 15cm (6in x 6in) pieces of the homespun fabric. Use a straight stitch and a 7mm ($^{1}/_{4}$in) seam allowance to join together all three to form a strip with the leftover skirt fabric in the centre, as shown in diagram 1. Press the seams toward the dress fabric.

Diagram 1

Fold the strip in half with right sides together, aligning the homespun ends so the fold is through the dress fabric. Leaving space for $^{1}/_{4}$in seam allowances, place the leg template on the fabric strip so that the bottom 5cm (2in) is placed on the outerskirt fabric (this will create the doll's shoes) as shown in diagram 2. Trace the leg template onto the fabric, then stitch, trim, and turn through in the same manner as for the body.

Stuff the body firmly with the fiberfill, then turn in 7mm ($^{1}/_{4}$in) at the lower opening and pin closed.

Stuff the legs firmly to the stuffing line. Bring the top raw edges together, matching seams and stitch closed.

Insert the legs 7mm ($^{1}/_{4}$in) into the body, making sure both legs are the same length.

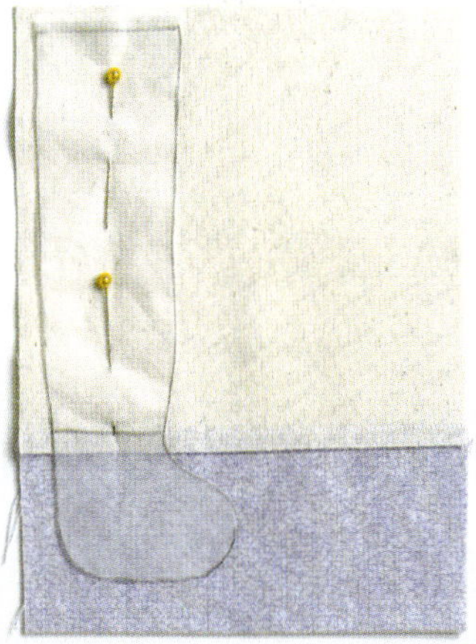

Diagram 2

Machine stitch the legs in place with a straight stitch through all layers. Tie two small bows for the shoes using the 3mm-wide ribbon. To attach the bows, hand stitch through the knot and the front seam line.

Stuff the arms firmly to the stuffing line and turn in 7mm (1/4in) at the top of each arm. Baste the openings and draw the threads to gather. Pin the arms to the shoulders and hand stitch in place.

Both the under and overskirts are made the same, though the overskirt is 2cm (3/4in) shorter. With right sides together, sew the two short sides of the overskirt fabric together. Neaten the raw edges then press. Repeat to create the underskirt. To sew the skirt hem, fold under 1cm (3/8in) and pin. Stabilise the fabric with tear-away stabiliser, then along each hemline, sew a different decorative stitch to hold the hem in place.

Join both skirt pieces together at the top. Then sew a small zig zag stitch over crochet cotton around the skirt top. Care must be taken not to catch the crochet cotton in the zig zag stitching. Pull the crochet cotton to gather the skirt. Place the skirt on the doll and draw the gathering threads tightly at the waist. Tie or stitch securely.

To create the doll's top, fold the doily in half, then into quarters, then into eighths to find the stitching lines shown in diagram 3.

Machine stitch along the one-eighth fold lines, starting from the outside edge and stopping 5cm (2in) from the central point. Using sharp scissors, carefully cut a small hole at the centre of the doily just large enough to fit over the doll's head.

Insert the doll's head through the opening and the arms through the sleeves. Handstitch the edge of the doily to the doll to stop it from unravelling.

Handstitch the small button onto the front of the doily.

To create the hair, loosely wrap the yarn around the length of a 13cm (5in) piece of cardboard until it is 7cm (3in) wide. Cut yarn at one end of the cardboard, then remove. Stitch across the centre of the yarn, through all layers to form a part. Make a few loops from the yarn and stitch to the forehead to form a fringe.

Place the centre of the hair on the middle of the doll's head and either stitch or glue in place. Tie the hair into pigtails, securing each with a ribbon bow.

Finally, using the pattern as a guide, draw the facial features using the fine point permanent fabric marker. Blush cheeks if desired. Start with the eyes – placing them half way down the centre of the face. Ensure they are level and not too wide apart. Then draw the nose and mouth and any other details, such as rosy cheeks or freckles.

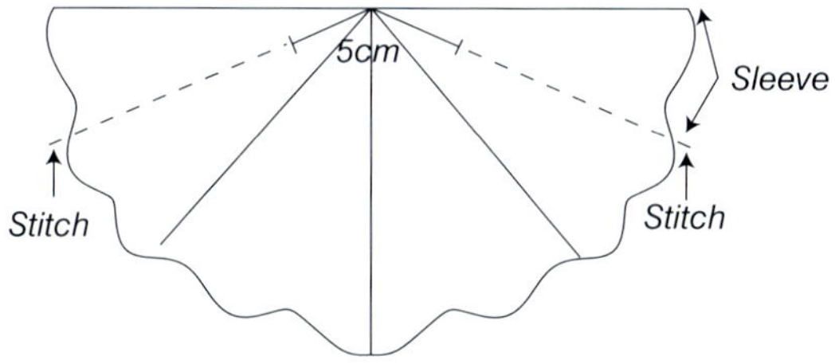

Diagram 3

SITTING ROOM

This elegant room has been created using warm golds, deep maroons and heritage greens. Not only are the colours lush, the textures of the fabrics add even more warmth and dimension.

Clever embellishments have been included in the handmade lampshade, but you can even purchase a lampshade and decorate it in the fashion described.

If you have considered trying freehand embroidery, then the landscape is the project for you. A manageable size, you will find it truly rewarding. The decorated tablecloth, cushion and footstool add to the setting, with elegant stitch building.

Tablecloth and Skirt

This elegant tablecloth and skirt have been designed for a small round table that is 54cm (21¼in) in diameter and 62cm (24½in) in height.

Requirements

- 4m x 115cm (157½in x 45⅓in) of main fabric
- 50cm x 115cm (20in x 45⅓in) of contrasting fabric
- 60cm x 60cm (23⅔in x 23⅔in) calico
- Large lace motifs or motifs cut from corded lace
- Embroidery thread to match the lace
- Thread to match the main fabric
- Tape measure
- Iron-on tear-away stabiliser
- Fabric stabiliser spray
- 25cm (10in) fusible webbing
- 4m (4⅜yds) piping cord no. 2
- Water-soluble marking pen
- Spray adhesive

Janome Accessories

- Bobbin Fill – J-208 or J-208-1
- Overlock Foot C – 822801001
- Walking Foot – 214873013
- Custom Crafted Foot F – 822804004
- Piping Foot – 200002101
- ¼in Seam Foot – 200008107

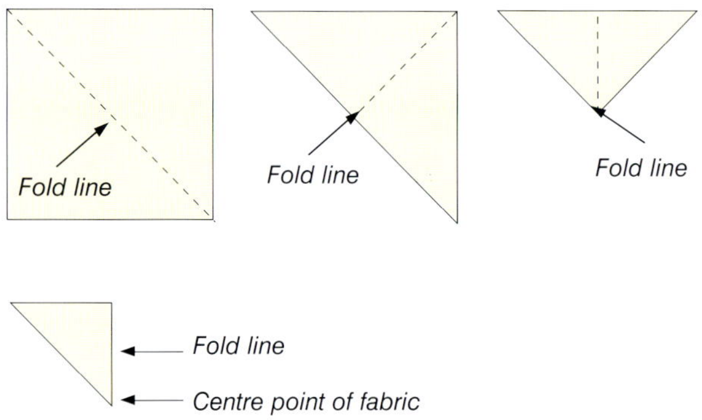

Diagram 1

Preparation

To make the circular table-topper cut one, 115cm (45⅓in) square from the main fabric.

Fold the square into a triangle, then again and once again as shown in diagram 1.

Measure the distance from the centre point of the fabric to the edge along the fold. Keeping the end of the tape measure on the centre point, move the tape across the fabric, marking off the same measurement at 5cm (2in) intervals with a water-soluble marking pen as shown in diagram 2.

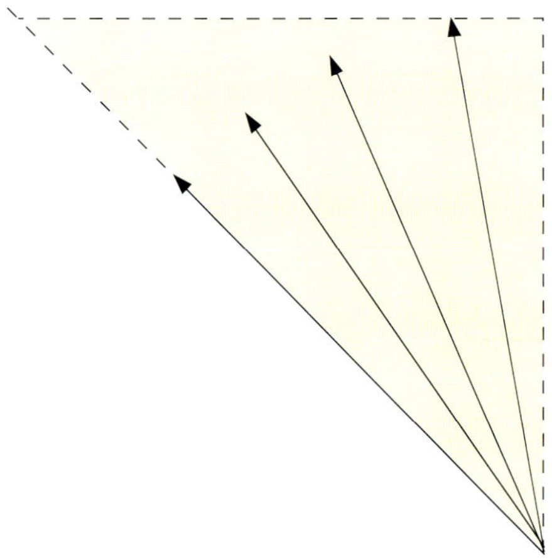

Diagram 2

Join these dots together and carefully cut along the line to create a circle of fabric. Mark the centre point of the fabric with a water soluble pen.

Construction

To over edge the circle and avoid fraying, select zig zag, length 1.5 and width 5. Attach the Overlock Foot C then stitch carefully around the raw edges of fabric.

Remove the fabric from the machine and using the centre point, measure and mark a 30.5cm x 30.5cm (12in x 12in) square in the centre of the fabric. This is the design area. Spray the design area with the fabric stabiliser, allow to dry and then press.

Cut a square of iron-on tear-away measuring 37cm x 37cm (14⅔in x 14⅔in) and apply it to the wrong side of the fabric so that it covers the underside of the design area.

In the design area, mark up the grid design shown in diagram 3 on the fabric with a water soluble pen. For this design 3.8cm (1½in) squares (10 across by 10 down) were used. Make sure the lines run parallel with the grain of the fabric.

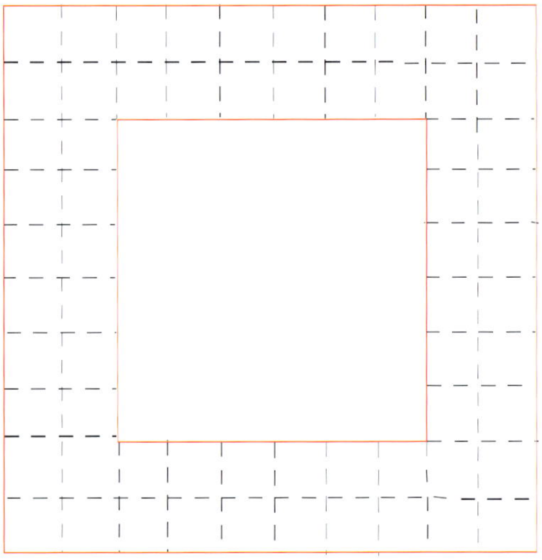

Diagram 3

Attach the Custom Crafted Foot F. Thread the machine with the desired embroidery thread and set the machine for satin stitch. Select zig zag, tension 2, length 0.3 and width 5. Satin stitch over each of the lines marked in broken lines on diagram 3, making sure the line is in the centre of the foot.

To make a locking stitch at the beginning and end of the stitching, set both the length and width controls to 0. Sew four or five stitches, then reset the machine to continue sewing the pattern or seam.

When the internal gridlines have been satin stitched, change the settings on the machine. Select stitch 30 and tension 2. The length is preset on this stitch and the width is the centre needle position. Sew as close as possible to each side of the satin stitch lines already sewn as shown in diagram 4.

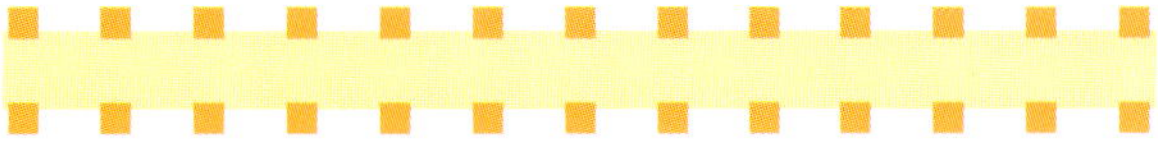

Diagram 4

If the iron-on tear-away paper is quickly disappearing from the back of the work, remove any residue and apply a new sheet.

To create the centre appliqué, cut a square of contrasting fabric measuring 23cm x 23cm (9in x 9in). Apply fusible webbing to the wrong side and peel off the paper backing. Position this onto the centre of the grid and iron into place.

Select zig zag, tension 2, length 0.3 and width 6. Sew around the square of contrast fabric (inner solid line on diagram 3), ensuring that the satin stitch completely covers the raw edges. Do the same around the outer square.

Select stitch 30 and tension 2 and stitch down each side of these satin stitched squares as was done previously for the internal gridlines.

The roses in the centre were cut from lace that had the flowers well defined by a satin stitched edge. Alternatively, ready made motifs can be bought or use an appropriate appliqué from a printed fabric.

To attach the roses, apply spray adhesive to the wrong side and position them onto the contrast fabric. As the spray adhesive is not permanent, it allows the pieces to be lifted off and rearranged as desired until the design is perfected.

After the arrangement is complete, set the machine to zig zag, tension 2, length 0.1, width 2 and foot pressure 2. Attach the Custom Crafted Foot F. Zig zag around the outer edges of the roses, using either a matching or invisible thread. Ensure that the swing of the needle only just goes over the edge of the motifs. Remove any stabiliser from the back of the fabric.

To create the piped hem, cut six, 25mm (1in) bias strips from the contrasting fabric and stitch them together to make bias tape.

Attach the Piping Foot and make the piping referring to the manufacturer's instructions included in the packaging for the piping foot.

Attach the piping to the edge of the tablecloth, raw edges together. Sew in exactly the same way as before except the cord should be in the left hand channel of the piping foot.

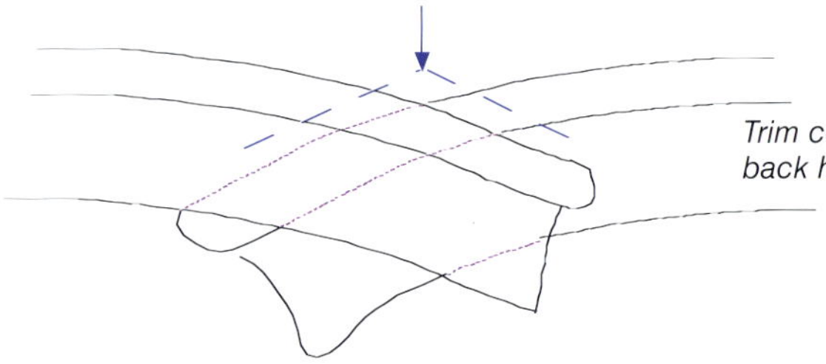

Diagram 5

To join the ends of the piping, trim back the piping cord inside both ends of the bias tape. Cross over the ends of the bias tape and sew through both layers of the tape as shown in diagram 5.

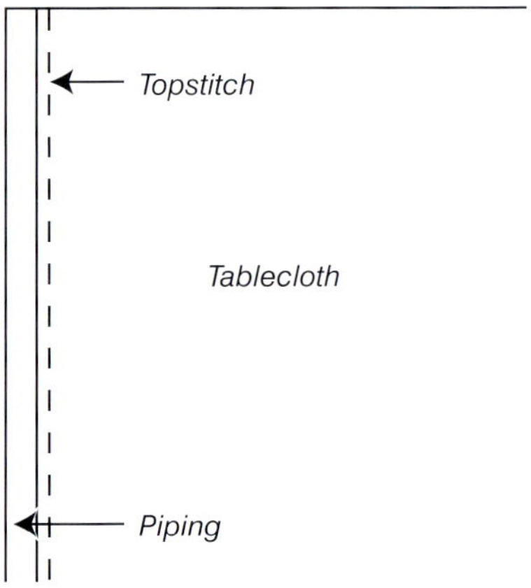

Diagram 6

Then, press the edges under to create a piped edge. To keep the tablecloth hem and the piping out of sight permanently, top stitch around the cloth, keeping the cord in the right hand channel and the needle in the centre position as shown in diagram 6.

Table skirt

Measure the height of the table. For this design the height of the table is 62cm (24½in). To this measurement, add 5cm (2in) for the hem and 1.5cm (⅔in) for the seam. Then, measure the circumference of the tabletop. For this design, the circumference is 169.5cm (66½in). To this measurement add one third for fullness. Now, cut this piece from the main fabric. For this design 68.5cm x 226cm (27⅓in x 89in) was cut.

Attach the ¼in Seam Foot and using the matching thread, join the two ends of the skirt with a French seam.

To achieve a neat finish on the hem of the skirt, measure and turn under 2.5cm (1in) of fabric. Press along the fold line for a crisp edge. Now, turn under another 2.5cm (1in) and pin in place. Use the matching thread and a straight stitch to sew the hem 2cm (¾in) from the edge.

Lay the calico on the tabletop and with a water-soluble pen, mark the table edges. Add an extra 1.5cm (¾in) for seam allowances. Using this measurement, cut out the circle of fabric.

Fold the circle in half, four times and pin mark the seam line with sixteen location points. Place the circle of fabric on the table-top wrong side up.

Fold the skirt in half the same number of times and pin mark the corresponding location points along the seam line. Pin the skirt to the tabletop matching location points. Between each location point there will be excess skirt fabric. At regular intervals, fold the excess fabric between the pins into a small pleat. This will create fullness.

After all the pleats have been pinned, use a straight stitch to sew the skirt to the calico circle. Press the seam allowance towards the centre of the tabletop. Then, using the ¼in Seam Foot as a guide, top stitch around the tabletop 7mm (¼in) from where the calico and skirt meet, then press.

Cushion

Create this delightful decorative cushion using a combination of patchwork and embroidery.

Requirements

- 60cm x 114cm (23½in x 45in) plain fabric
- 35cm x 114cm (14in x 45in) contrast fabric
- 5cm (2in) patterned fabric for patchwork
- 5cm (2in) coordinating fabric for patchwork
- 25cm x 25cm (10in x 10in) patterned fabric for centre appliqué
- 35cm x 30cm (14in x 12in) fusible webbing
- 60cm x 150cm (23½in x 59in) iron-on interfacing
- 80cm x 90cm (31½in x 35½in) iron-on Pellon
- 3 coordinating embroidery thread colours (matt gold, dark green, maroon)
- Monofilament thread
- 1 reel of maroon thread for cording
- 1 reel of thread to match the contrast fabric
- Iron-on tear-away stabiliser
- 2m x 4mm (78½in x ⅓in) silk ribbon
- 2m (78½in) piping cord no. 2
- 2m (78½in) piping cord no. 4
- 5 decorative buttons
- 2B pencil
- Rotary cutter and mat

Janome Accessories

- Bobbin Fill – J-208 or J-208-1
- Ribbon Sequin Foot – 2000025100
- Piping Foot – 200002101
- ¼in Seam Foot – 200008107
- Overlock Foot C – 822801001
- Custom Crafted Foot F – 822804004
- Blind Foot G – 825817009
- Cording Foot H – 820819006
- Red tip needle – 990314000
- Denim needle – 990416000

Preparation

Cut a strip of Pellon to measure 6.4cm x 85cm (2½in x 33½in). This is the padding for the contrast fabric on the back of the cushion. Iron the interfacing, then the Pellon onto the back of the plain fabric.

Cut the following pieces from this plain fabric, following the diagram on the pattern sheet: four 36.8cm x 8.9cm (14½in x 3½in) strips, two 22.9cm x 44.5cm (9½in x 17½in) strips and one 36.8cm x 36.8cm (14½in x 14½in) square.

Cut the two chosen patchwork fabrics into 3.8cm (1½in) wide strips. Using the ¼in Seam Foot, make four, four-patch blocks for the corners and one nine-patch block for the centre.

Iron the interfacing, then Pellon onto the back of each four-patch block. Iron fusible webbing onto the back of the nine-patch and trim away the 7mm (¼in) seam allowance.

Take the 25cm (9⅞in) square of patterned fabric and iron fusible webbing onto the back. Draw a 20.3cm (8in) circle onto the fabric. Now, draw a 15.3cm (6in) circle inside the first circle. Carefully cut along the lines of both circles to create the circular appliqué shape for the middle of the cushion. Set aside.

To create the piping, cut two pieces measuring 3.2cm x 115cm (1½in x 45in) from the contrast fabric. Stitch the two pieces together to make the piping tape. Attach the Piping Foot and using the No. 2 piping cord make the piping referring to the instructions in the package.

From the contrast fabric, cut a further two pieces measuring 5cm x 115cm (2in x 45in), stitch together and using the No. 4 piping cord make the piping for the cushion edges.

Still using the contrast fabric, cut two, 12.7cm x 44.5cm (5in x 17½in) lengths to be used for the button closures at the back. Iron the interfacing onto the back of these two pieces, then fold both in half lengthwise and iron. Now, cut two strips of iron-on Pellon measuring 6.35cm x 44.45cm (2½in x 17½in). Unfold the fabric and iron the Pellon onto one side of the interfacing on each piece as shown in diagram 1.

Construction

To create the sashings, thread the sewing machine with the matt gold embroidery thread. Select stitch 40, tension 2, length 2.5 and width 5.0.

Attach the Ribbon/Sequin Foot to the machine. Thread with the 4mm silk ribbon and sew down the centre of each panel.

Thread the machine with the green embroidery thread and decorate two of the sashing panels. Select stitch 52, tension 2, length 0.3 and width 7.0.

Now, attach the Custom Crafted Foot F to the machine and sew down either side of the silk ribbon.

Change to the maroon embroidery thread. Select stitch 67 and sew alongside stitch 39.

To decorate the other two sashing panels, select stitch 93, tension 2, length 2.5 and width 7.0.

Sew down either side of the silk ribbon on the last two panels. (Stitch settings will only be given from now on if they differ from the standard settings.)

Select stitch 45 and sew alongside stitch 93. Then, trim all four panels so they measure 6.4cm x 30.5cm (2½in x 12in).

To make the centre panel, remove the paper backing from the patterned circle previously made. Place the circle onto the centre of the 36.8cm (14½in) square plain fabric piece. Iron into place.

Thread the matt gold embroidery thread through the machine, then select stitch 26. Sew carefully around both the inner and outer edge of the circle.

Change to the maroon embroidery thread, select stitch 76, and sew around the new outer edge created by the first embroidery thread. Select stitch 47 and sew around the new inner edge.

Change to the green embroidery thread, select stitch 44 and sew one star above the peak of each stitch 76 placed on the outer edge of the circle. Now, place the

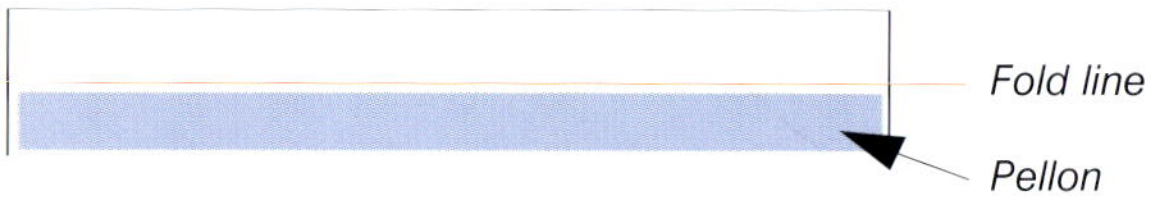

Diagram 1

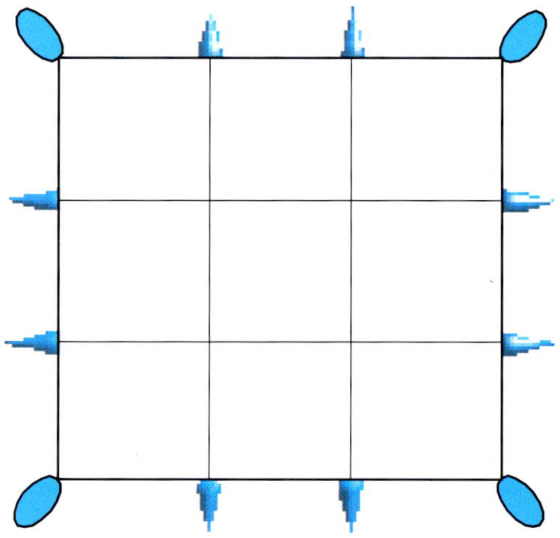

Diagram 2

nine-patch block onto the centre of the design area and iron into place.

Change to the matt gold embroidery thread, select stitch 26 and sew around the edge of the nine-patch to appliqué into place. Change to the green embroidery thread and select stitch 51, length 0.3 and width 7.0. Sew one pattern only at an angle on each corner as shown in diagram 2.

Now, select stitch 53, length 0.3 and width 7.0. Sew one pattern only at the two seam lines on the edge of the patch as shown in diagram 2.

To complete the nine-patch design, change to the maroon embroidery thread and sew a star on the end of each pattern using stitch 44 as shown in diagram 3.

To decorate each of the corners of the centre panel, sew diagonally across each corner, working from the centre out to the corner with each stitch 1.3cm ($\frac{1}{2}$in) apart. Stitch the

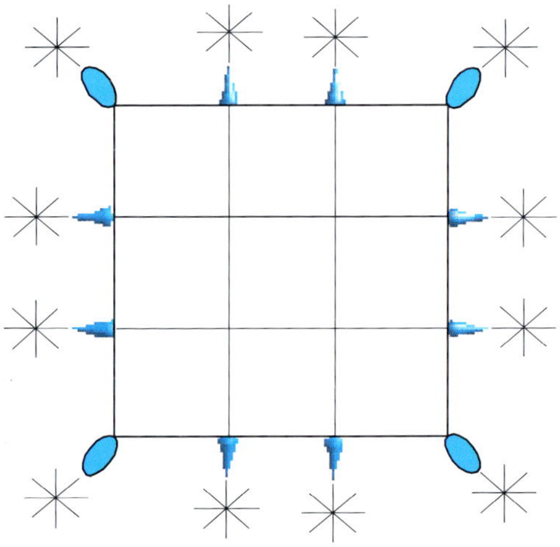

Diagram 3

patterns following the stitch sequence 30, 85, 30, 80, 30, 85, 30. When sewing stitch 30, thread the machine with the monofilament thread (this is not invisible thread but a fine, transparent, monofilament thread). Increase the top tension to approximately 4 or 5. This will give stitch 30 a hand quilted look.

When complete, trim the centre panel so that it measures 31.75cm x 31.75cm ($12\frac{1}{2}$in x $12\frac{1}{2}$in).

To construct the cushion back, mark the two back sections of the cushion with five lines, spaced 7.6cm (3in) apart, as shown in diagram 4.

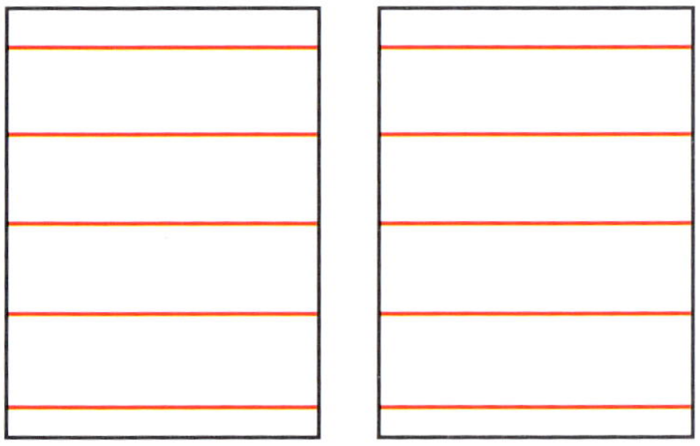

Diagram 4

Thread the machine with the matt gold embroidery thread and select stitch 46. Attach Cording Foot H, then thread one strand of the cording thread into each channel. Keeping the guide lines in the centre of the foot, couch the threads into place.

Now, thread the machine with the maroon embroidery thread and select stitch 70. Change back to Custom Crafted Foot H and sew down each side of the cording. Trim the edges.

To create the button bands at the back, thread the machine and the bobbin with good quality sewing thread to match the contrast fabric. Select stitch 7 and attach Overlock Foot C. Overcast the long edge of each band that has only interfacing on the back.

Diagram 5

IT'S SEW EASY

PATTERN SHEET

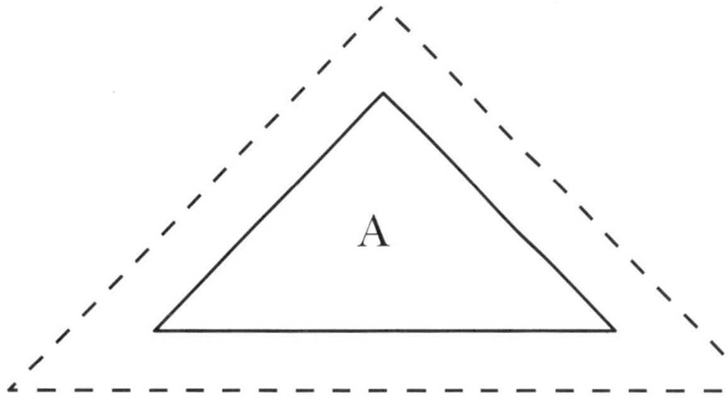

Placemats and Director's Chairs

Outdoor Setting

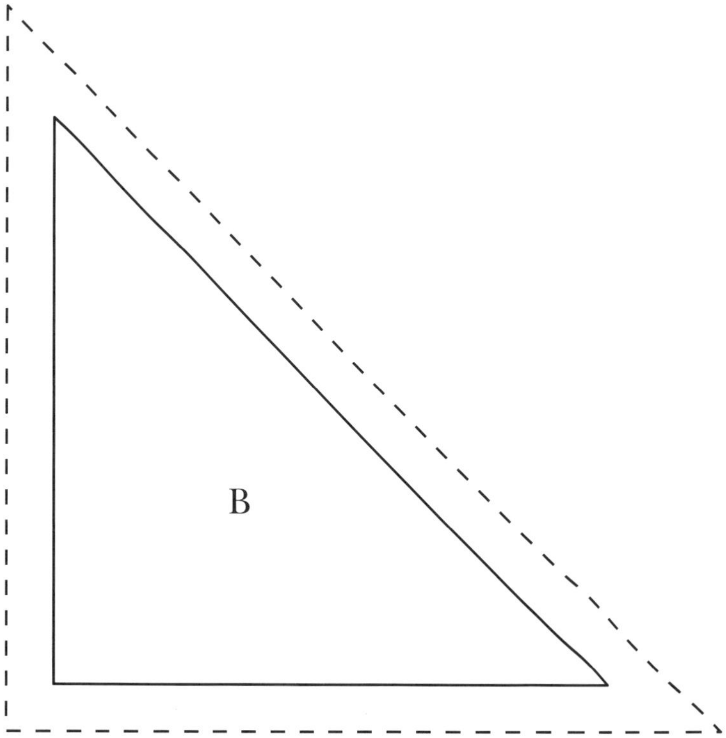

Placemats and
Director's Chairs

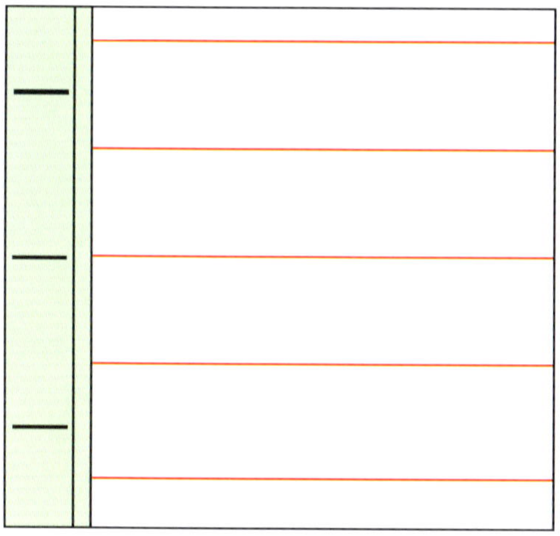

Diagram 6

Select the straight stitch, centre the needle position and attach the 1/4in Seam Foot. Stitch together the long edge of the decorated back section with the interfacing and Pellon-backed long edge of the button band, as shown in diagram 5.

Fold the button band along the fold line bringing the overcast edge to the back. Change the settings to length 2.6 and width 0.5. Attach Blind Foot G.

Topstitch the button band along the seam line, ensuring the guide on Blind Foot G stays on the seam and catching in the overcast edge underneath the stitching.

Make five buttonholes in line with the decorative stitches, in one of the button bands. Overlap the two button bands (with the buttonholes on the top) and stitch across the bottom and top edges to hold together during construction, as shown in diagram 6.

Attach the Piping Foot to the machine and stitch the no.2 covered piping to the left and right sides of the centre block. To do this, place the cord into the right hand channel of the piping foot, so the stitching will be on the left side of the cord through the casing and centre panel. Stitch the length of the casing strip, keeping the edges even and the cord tucked into the fold, as shown in diagram 7.

Place the sashings and centre panel with piping, right sides together and sew close to the piping through all the layers.

Diagram 7

Diagram 8

Attach the same size piping to the top and bottom of the joined pieces and the short sides of the remaining sashings using the same method as for the centre panel, as shown in diagram 8.

Then, stitch a four-patch block to each end of the unattached sashes as shown in diagram 9.

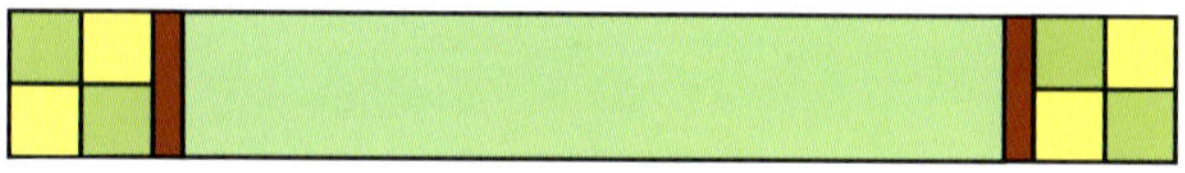

Diagram 9

Stitch one of the sashes to the top and one to the bottom of the centre panel to complete the front of the cushion as shown in diagram 10. Now stitch the no.4 covered piping cord all the way around the edge of the cushion front.

Select length 2.8 and width 3.0 then insert the denim needle. Place together the right sides of the back and front panels and sew close to the piping through all the layers. Trim the seams and corners. Turn the cushion through to the right side, sew the buttons into place and press.

Diagram 10

Lampshade

Create this charming lampshade using beading, braid, ribbons, fabric and a little imagination.

Requirements

- 50cm x 115cm (19½in x 45½in) plain silk fabric
- 25.5cm (10in) dome lampshade frame
- One card of 12mm x 5m (½in x 5½yds) bias binding
- 1m x 9.5cm (1⅛yds x 3½in) satin-edged organza ribbon
- 1m (1⅛yds) graduated silk wire-edged ribbon
- 1m (1⅛yds) beaded fringing
- 2m (2¼yds) lampshade braid
- Quick-drying craft glue
- Glass headed pins
- Fabric scissors
- A3 paper or Vilene for pattern
- Tear-away stabiliser
- Embroidery thread
- 2B pencil

Janome Accessories

- Overlock Foot C – 822801001
- Custom Crafted Foot F – 822804004
- ¼in Seam Foot – 200008107

Method

To make the pattern, place the wire frame of the lampshade onto a piece of A3 paper or Vilene. Use the pencil to draw around the outside of the wires on one segment of the frame. Tip the frame to accurately draw the shape at the top. Then, roll the frame sideways and draw around the second segment of the frame in the same way, to create the pattern as shown in diagram 1.

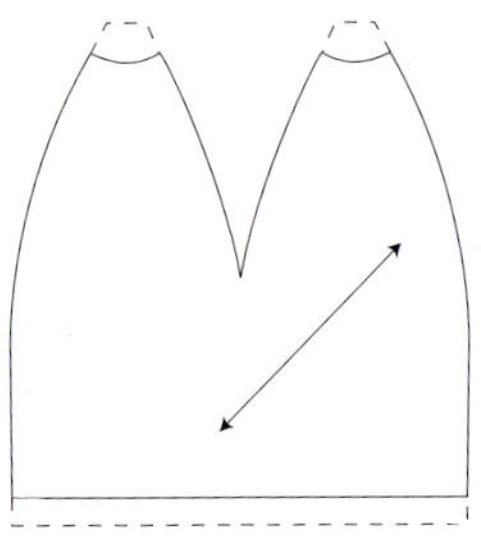

Diagram 1

Add 3cm (1½in) at both the top and bottom of the pattern to allow for stretch and turnings. There is no need to add a seam allowance to the sides of the pattern as there will be sufficient fabric when it is stretched over the frame. Mark the grain line on the paper pattern at a 45-degree angle to the base line as shown in diagram 1. Pin the paper pattern onto the plain fabric, matching the grain line of the pattern with the grain of the fabric. From the fabric, cut four shade pieces.

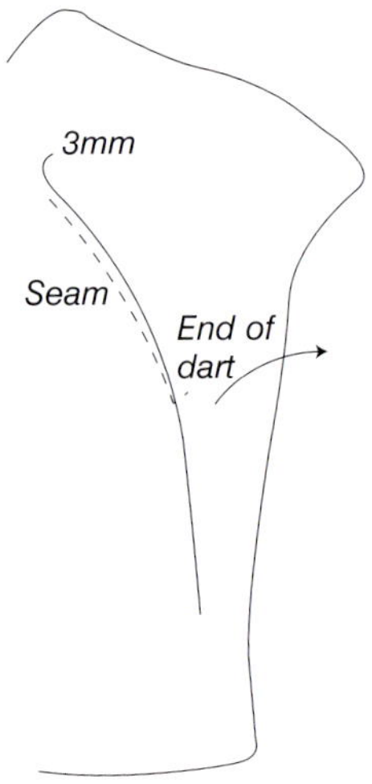

Diagram 2

Construction

The first step is to sew the darts. On each segment, pin together the (split) middle section in the fabric. Starting at the top of the shade fabric, sew a 3mm (⅛in) seam that tails off the end of the dart as shown in diagram 2. Repeat for the other three pattern pieces.

Pin together all the side seams and using the ¼in Seam Foot and a long straight stitch, sew one row of stitching. Test the fit of the shade on the frame with the wrong sides facing out. If the shade does not fit properly, pin mark the seams or darts that need to be restitched. Take the shade off the frame and sew along the pin markings, using a normal stitch if restitching the darts or a long straight stitch for the seams. Then, test the fit on the frame again and make any further necessary adjustments. When the shade fits properly, sew the side seams using a normal stitch length.

When sewing the seams for a lampshade, it is a good idea to sew a second (reinforcement) seam just inside the first. This prevents the seams from splitting when the fabric is stretched over the frame. Just be sure to check the shade fits properly before sewing the reinforcement seam.

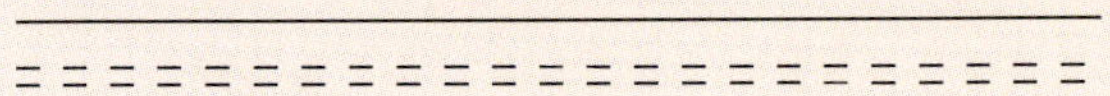

Diagram 3

When the side seams have been double stitched, trim the seam allowance to 3mm (⅛in), except for the last 5cm (2½in) at the top, as shown in diagram 4. This extra fabric will be used to turn the top edge over on the frame.

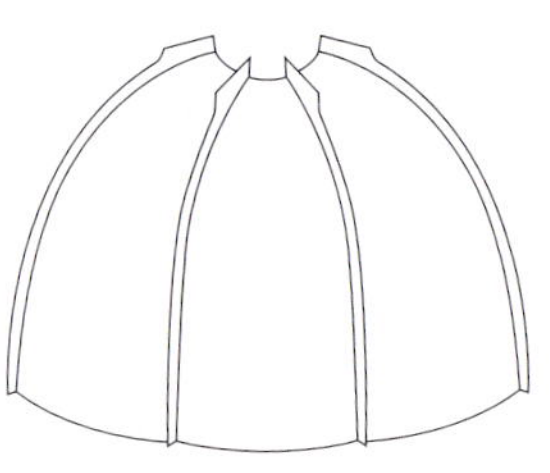

Diagram 4

Tightly wrap the lampshade bias around the entire wire frame of the lampshade and stitch to secure. The fabric is now ready to be attached to

the frame. Stretch the shade fabric over the frame, matching the seams and darts to the vertical wire struts. Pin the fabric to the frame at regular intervals.

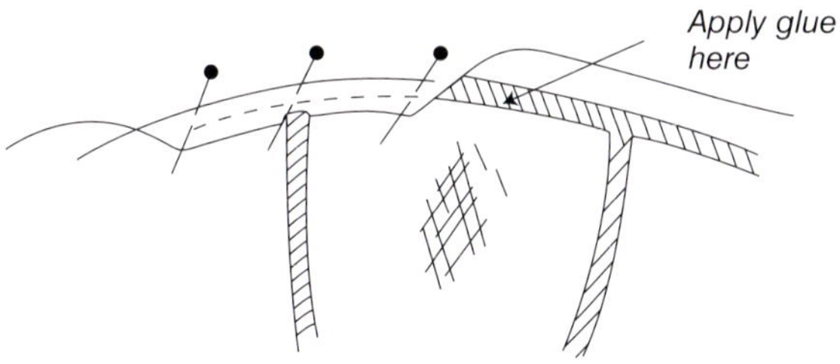

Diagram 5

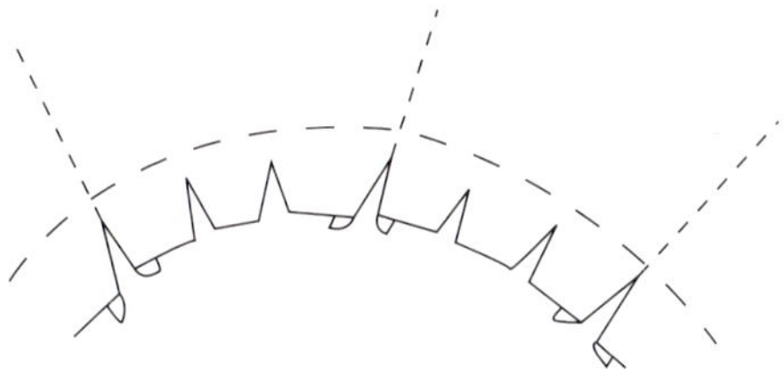

Diagram 6

Pin through both the fabric and bias covering to ensure an even stretch. Now, trim the extra turning fabric at the bottom of the shade (the hem) to 1.5cm ($^5/_8$in).

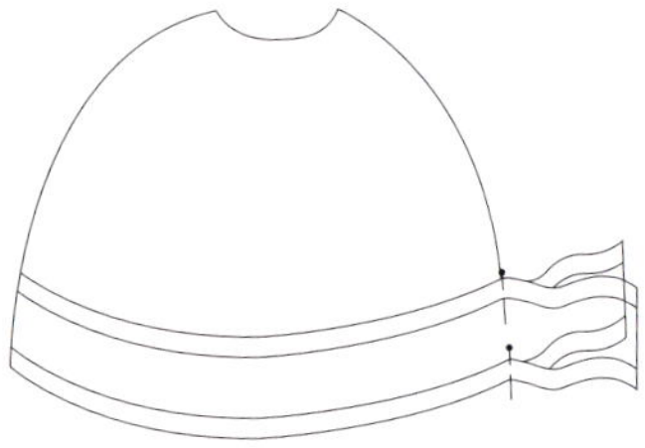

Diagram 7

Sparingly apply the craft glue to the inside edge of the bias covering on the lower rim of the frame, taking great care not to get glue on the shade fabric, as shown in diagram 5.

Attach and pin the shade fabric to the glued frame one section at a time. Allow the glue to dry completely before moving on to the next step.

When the glue has dried, trim the top opening to 2cm (3/4in) from the top of the frame. Unpick 1.5cm (5/8in) of stitching from the top of the shade fabric. Then clip the fabric around the frame top where the lampshade supports are attached so the fabric can be neatly turned in as shown in diagram 6.

Glue and pin the top of the shade fabric to the frame using the same method as for lower rim.

Finishing

Now it is time to decorate the lampshade cover. Place the satin-edged organza ribbon around the base of the lamp so that it fits snugly, and pin the ends of the ribbon together as shown in diagram 7.

Take the ribbon off the lampshade, and using a normal stitch, double stitch the ribbon along the pin marking. Press the satin edges of the ribbon over towards the centre.

This lampshade has a circumference of 81cm, so nine prairie points at the top and nine at the bottom will be used. Mark the folded satin edges on the right side, at 9cm intervals as shown in diagram 8.

The prairie points will be made from the wire-edged silk ribbon. For this design nine have been made so that the tip is light and nine with the tip dark. From the ribbon cut 18, 5cm (2½in) pieces. Fold in two corners of each piece as shown in diagram 9, ensuring nine have a light tip and nine have a dark tip. Then press each point. Pin the pieces to the satin-edged organza ribbon, slipping them slightly under the folded satin edge and centring them with the markings made earlier. Pin into place. Make sure those with the dark tips are pinned to the bottom of the satin-edged organza and those with the light tips are pinned to the top. Set the machine to straight stitch, centre needle position, length 3.0 and attach the Overlock Foot C. This foot has a guide that will keep the stitches close to the edge as indicated in diagram 10.

Apply the tear-away stabiliser to the back of the satin-edged organza ribbon. Thread the machine with a decorative embroidery thread that will enhance the colours already used. Select stitch 50, tension 2, length 0.3 and width 5.

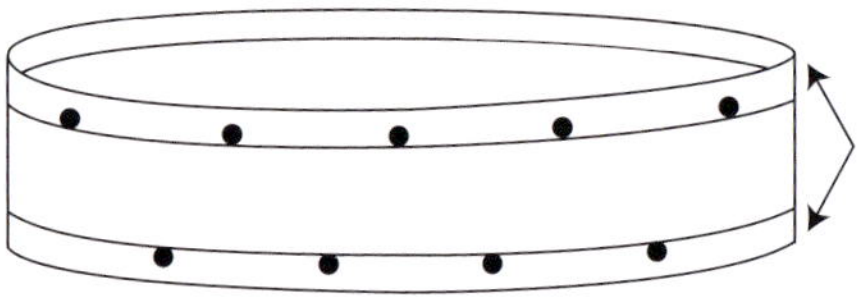

Diagram 8

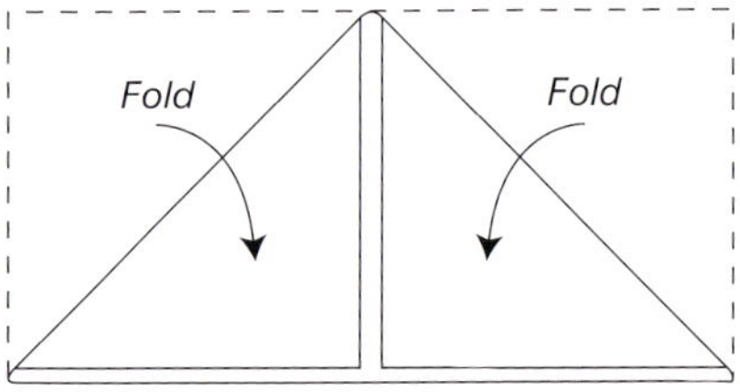

Diagram 9

Attach the Custom Crafted Foot F.

Sew the decorative stitch onto the satin edging ensuring that the needle swings off the edge and on to the prairie points thus hiding the ribbon edge as shown in diagram 11. Repeat for the other side. Remove the tear-away stabiliser and press.

Fit the decorative strip back onto the base of the lampshade and using a light tacking stitch attach it to the bottom edge of the shade (this will be covered later).

To attach the beaded fringe, turn the lampshade upside down. Working from the inside, glue and pin the tape of the beaded fringe to the inside edge of the shade base. This step is easier if the beads are hung over the edge, on the outside, out of the way. Allow the glue to dry before turning the shade the right way up.

Finally, glue the lampshade braid all around the bottom edge of the lampshade to cover any joins or stitching. Attach more of the braid (gluing only at the wire struts) to the top edge of the decorative strip so that it fits snugly around the lampshade. Then glue more braid around the top edge of the shade.

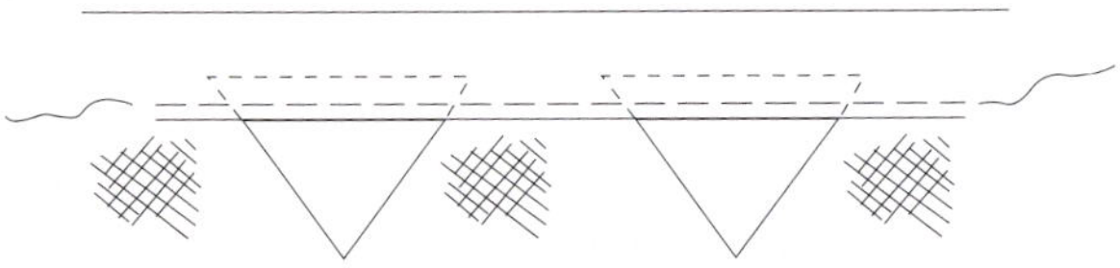

Diagram 10

Diagram 11

Freehand
EMBROIDERED LANDSCAPE

Create an attractive landscape picture using freehand embroidery techniques.

Preparation

Pre-wash the calico and press. Using the pencil, lightly rule a frame onto one of the calico squares. For this design the frame measured 27cm x 18.5cm (10⅝in x 7⅓in). The area inside the frame is where the embroidery will be worked.

Using watercolour pencils or paints, colour the landscape background. To prevent bleeding, allow each colour to dry before continuing. Once completed, press the fabric to set the paint.

Iron the fusible interfacing onto the back of the calico. This will stabilise the fabric and prevent stretching. Using the pencil, lightly sketch the details of the landscape from the pattern sheet, including the outline of the tree trunk and branches, the fence and the height and shape of the bushes.

Place this prepared fabric into the 20cm (8in) embroidery hoop so that it is drum tight. Stretch the

OUTDOOR SETTING

Looking for something to make for the man in your life? Then here it is! The projects for the outdoor setting include an apron, mitt and hat that are sure to look great, as well as being practical.

The pretty placemats and serviettes add a bright accent and the bread roll holder, cutlery holder and serviette rings all add to the setting.

Stitch building, Seminole patchwork, general patchwork piecing, simple appliqué and general sewing skills are all used to great effect and the results are rewarding.

Placemats

Finished size

40cm x 30cm (15¾in x 12in)
(The following instructions make four)

Requirements

- 1.5m (60in) plain fabric
- 15cm (6in) plain fabrics (to match serviettes)
- 15cm (6in) patterned fabric
- Small quantity of two plain fabrics (colour 1 and colour 2) for the patchwork basket
- Floral fabric with leaves and flowers to be used for the appliqué – or cut templates
- Paper, cardboard or plastic for templates
- 15cm (6in) fusible webbing
- Water-soluble marking pen
- Tear-away stabiliser
- Cording thread to match the 1.5m (60in) plain fabric
- 70cm (28in) Iron-on Pellon
- Embroidery thread to match the main fabric
- Embroidery threads for appliqué
- Embroidery threads to match plain fabrics
- Sewing thread for construction and quilting

Janome Accessories

- ¼in Seam Foot – 200008107
- Custom Crafted Foot F – 822804004
- Cording Foot H – 820819006
- Walking Foot – 214873013

Method

From the pattern sheet, make templates for all five shapes (these shapes can also be used for the director's chair backs) – a 7mm (¼in) seam allowance has been included. From each of the four background fabrics, cut one of template E, two of template B, two of template C and two of template D.

Cut 18 A triangles from the following fabrics:
12 from the patterned fabric, four from colour 1 and two from colour 2 fabric.

With ¼in Seam Foot, join all the patchwork pieces, using the block construction diagram as a positioning guide. Complete all four placemat centres and press.

Iron the fusible webbing to the back of the flower and leaf fabric. Alternatively, use templates from the pattern sheet to cut shapes. Cut out 12 flowers and 16 leaves. Remove the backing paper and position three flowers and four leaves on the completed blocks. Press in place.

Using Custom Crafted Foot F, stitch 26, width 2, length 2, stitch around each of the flowers and leaves.

From the patterned fabric cut eight 21.5cm x 6.5cm (8½in x 2½in) strips. With a water-soluble marking pen, draw a line down the centre of each strip and use the buttonhole guide on the pattern sheet to mark the buttonhole positions. Using tear-away to stabilise, buttonhole each of the fabric strips.

Cut two 22.5cm x 2.5cm (9in x 1in) strips for each placemat from the plain background fabrics. Fold a 12mm (½in) turning to the back on both sides lengthways and press.

Attach the Cording Foot H and place the cording thread into the two outside cording slots.

Select stitch 45, thread the machine with embroidery thread matching the colour of the strip and with tear-away stabiliser, sew down the centre of all strips.

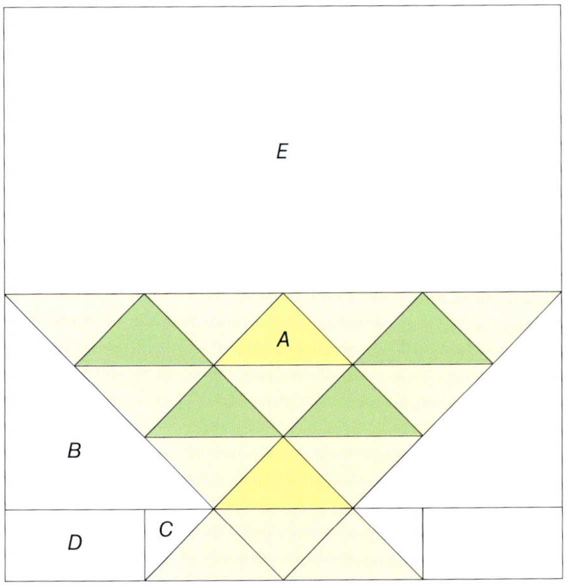

Block construction diagram

Thread the completed strips through the buttonholes. Using the 1/4in Seam Foot, attach the patterned strips to the appliquéd and patchworked centres. Press.

From main fabric, cut eight 6.5cm x 21.5cm (2 1/2in x 8 1/2in) strips. Sew a strip of the plain fabric to either side of the patterned strip on each placemat. Press seams.

From main fabric cut eight strips 6.5cm x 43cm (2 1/2in x 17in). Attach these strips to the top and bottom edges of each of the placemats. Press seams.

Cut four pieces of the Iron-on Pellon to match the size of the placemats and following the manufacturer's instructions, press onto the placemats, taking care that the adhesive does not come in contact with the iron.

From the main fabric cut four pieces to the size of the placemats and pin the layers together.

Attach the Walking Foot and Quilting Guide to your machine. Stitch in the ditch around the patchwork centre. Using the quilting bar as a guide, sew two rows of stitching approximately 1.5cm (5/8in) apart around the placemat, on the main fabric.

From the main fabric cut 6.5cm (2 1/2in) strips for the placemat bindings. Then join all the pieces together on the bias to make one length. Press in half, wrong sides together and sew the binding to the right side of each placemat, mitring the corner. Fold the binding to the back and slipstitch in place.

Serviettes AND Serviette Rings

Either use fabric printed with flowers and leaves as the appliqué shapes or cut shapes from solid fabrics using the templates.

Requirements

- 4, 45cm (18in) plain fabrics
- Floral fabric with leaves and flowers that can be used for appliqué – or use templates
- 10cm (4in) fusible webbing
- Embroidery threads for appliqué
- Sewing thread for construction

Janome Accessories

- Custom Crafted Foot F – 822804004

Method

Cut a 42cm square from each of the four coloured fabrics. Turn under a double 7mm (1/4in) hem on each side of each square and sew using matching sewing thread.

Iron fusible webbing to the back of the floral and leaf fabric. Cut out four flowers and eight leaves.

Remove the backing paper from the fabric and position one flower and two leaves to the corner of each serviette and press.

Using Custom Crafted Foot F and matching embroidery threads, select stitch 26, width 3 length 2 and appliqué around the flowers and leaves.

Serviette Rings

Requirements

- Cardboard roll cut into four, 2.5cm (1in) lengths
- 10cm (4in) plain fabric
- 10cm (4in) patterned fabric
- Embroidery threads
- Tear-away stabiliser
- Water-soluble marking pen
- Craft glue

Janome Accessories

- Custom Crafted Foot F – 822804004
- 1/4in Seam Foot – 200008107

Method

From the plain fabric, cut four pieces measuring 5cm x 20cm (2in x 8in).

Draw a line with the water-soluble marking pen down the centre of each of the fabric pieces.

Change the embroidery thread on each strip to match the colours of the serviettes. Select stitch 26 and, using tear-away stabiliser, sew the decorative pattern along the line ending with one full pattern.

Drop the needle to the lowest position, turn the work and stitch a second row of stitching, so the pattern is mirror-reversed.

Re-cut the decorated fabric strips to 2.5cm (1in) wide with the two rows of decorative stitching centred.

Cut eight pieces of patterned fabric 20cm x 5cm (8in x 2in). Using the 1/4in Seam Foot, sew a strip of patterned fabric either side of the decorative stitching. Trim each piece to a width of 6cm (2½in) and neaten the outside raw edges.

Measure around the cardboard roll and stitch the fabric in a circle to match the measurement. Trim the seam and position the circle of fabric onto the cardboard roll.

Using craft glue, turn the fabric edges to the inside of the roll, press firmly in place and allow to dry.

Director's Chairs

Requirements

- Director's chairs with a removable back
- One patterned fabric for the flower baskets
- Two plain fabrics for the flower baskets
- Floral fabric with leaves and flowers that can be used for appliqué – or use templates
- 15cm (6in) fusible webbing
- Embroidery threads for appliqué

Janome Accessories

- 1/4in Seam Foot – 200008107
- Custom Crafted Foot F – 822804004

Method

These instructions are for one chair back.

From the pattern sheet, make a template for shape A of the flower basket from the templates for the placemats – a 7mm (1/4in) seam allowance has been included.

Using the triangle template, cut out 12 from the patterned fabric, four from the one plain fabric and two from the other plain fabric. Using the 1/4in Seam Foot, join the triangles.

Press all the seams. Iron fusible webbing to the back of the patchwork piece. Trim off the 7mm (1/4in) seam allowance from the outer edges.

Remove the backing paper and position the patchwork piece to the chair back. Iron in place.

Using the Custom Crafted Foot F and stitch 26, width 3 length 2, appliqué the patchwork piece along the raw edges.

Iron the fusible webbing to the floral and leaf fabrics. Cut out three flowers and four leaves. Peel off backing paper, position flowers and leaves and iron in place. Appliqué around each flower and leaf with matching embroidery threads.

Decorate the required number in the same manner and place the finished chair backs back onto the frames.

Chef's Hat, Apron and Oven Mitt

Requirements

- Kwik Sew Pattern 2284 and 2311
- 2m (2 3/16yds) main fabric
- 50cm (20in) each of four contrasting fabrics
- Sewing thread
- Water-soluble marking pen
- Bias binding tape 25mm (1in) wide
- 40cm (15 3/4in) square cotton batting
- Basting spray
- 1.2m (1 5/16yds) of 5mm (1/2in) wide piping cord
- 10cm (4in) hook and loop fastener
- Rotary cutter, mat and ruler

Janome Accessories

- 1/4in Seam Foot – 200008107
- Piping Foot – 200002101
- Walking Foot – 214873013

Apron

Method

Following the manufacturer's directions, cut the apron pieces from the main fabric using the Kwik Sew pattern.

To make the decorative Seminole strip, cut the following fabrics.
From the main fabric and the four contrasting fabrics cut,
Two 3cm x 112cm (1 1/4in x 44in) strips in blue
Two 3cm x 112cm (1 1/4in x 44in) strips in red
Two 3cm x 112cm (1 1/4in x 44in) strips in green
Two 3cm x 112cm (1 1/4in x 44in) strips in yellow
One 3cm x 112cm (1 1/4in x 44in) strip in black

Attach the 1/4in Seam Foot and stitch the fabric strips together in order of preference, matching the same sequence on both sides of the black centre strip.

Press all seams to one side and crosscut into 3.8cm (1 1/2in) strips.

Stitch these strips together, off-set each one by one square. This will build up a zig zag effect at the edges as shown in diagram 1.

Cut this Seminole strip in half and join the two angled ends together to make a longer strip as shown in diagram 2.

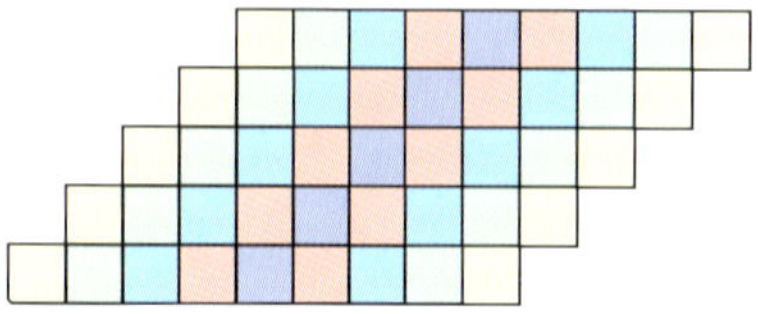

Diagram 1

Trim the top and bottom of the strip to make a straight edge. Be sure to leave a 7mm (1/4in) seam allowance for attaching the strip to the apron. This is the Seminole strip.

Measure the depth of the Seminole strip – it should be 10.8cm (4 1/4in) in depth. Using a water-soluble marking pen, draw a line at this measurement plus 1cm (1/2in) above the lower raw edge of the apron.

With right sides together, place the Seminole strip along the drawn line and stitch in place, being careful to stitch through the points of each square in the top row of the Seminole.

Fold the strip to the right side (towards the lower edge of the apron) and press.

Mark the position for the Seminole strip at the top edge of the apron in the same manner and sew in place.

The upper and lower edges of the apron have been self-bound with the apron fabric.

Fold and press the raw edges of the top and bottom edges of the apron to the front. Turn and stitch a hem encasing the raw edges of the Seminole strip.

Using the 25mm (1in) bias binding, bind the sides of the apron. Attach the apron ties to the neck and sides and press.

Oven Mitt

Cut out oven mit pattern pieces from the main fabric. Cut five 25.4cm x 3.8cm (10in x 1 1/2in) coloured strips and stitch together in the same order as the Seminole strip for the apron.

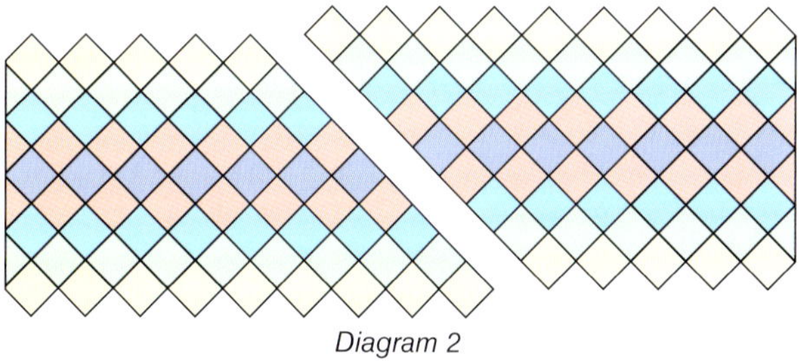

Diagram 2

Press the seams to one side. Cut a piece of batting the size of the strip and spray-baste to the stitched strips.

Add this piece to the lower edge of the mitt front in the same manner as the Seminole strips were added to the apron. Fold to the right side and press.

Using the walking foot, stitch in the ditch between the strips.

Construct the palm of the mitt following the pattern instructions, using the walking foot when stitching the quilting lines.

To complete the mitt, pin the wrong sides together and add the 25mm (1in) bias binding to all the mitt edges.

Chef's Hat

Cut 3.8cm (1½in) strips from the coloured contrasting fabrics and using the ¼in seam foot, sew the strips together. Press the seams to one side.

Cross cut into 3.8cm (1½in) strips and join the pieces to create two strips approximately 71cm (28in) long.

Join the two strips together, offsetting the squares one colour to the right. This gives the appearance of diagonal squares in a checkerboard pattern.

Make the hat following the pattern instructions, adding bias binding piping to the upper and lower edge of the patched hat band.

Cutlery
ROLL

This cutlery holder makes use of the same design elements as those shown in the chair backs and placemats.

Requirements

- 60cm (24in) plain fabric
- 35cm (14in) iron-on Pellon
- Small quantity of patterned fabric
- 2 plain fabrics
- 2 flowers for appliqué – or use templates
- Sewing thread for construction
- Embroidery threads
- Water-soluble marking pen
- Small piece of fusible webbing
- Rotary cutter, mat and ruler
- 1.6/70 Twin needle

Janome Accessories

- Custom Crafted Foot F – 822804004
- 1/4in Seam Foot – 200008107

Method

From the plain fabric cut,
One 58cm x 63cm (23in x 24in) piece for the cutlery holder
One 58cm x 16cm (23in x 6in) piece for the cutlery divider
Two 30cm x 6cm (12in x 2 1/2in) strips for the ties

Cut one piece of Pellon measuring 32cm x 58cm (12 1/2in x 23in)

Hem one long edge of the cutlery divider fabric. Allowing a 1cm (1/2in) seam allowance at either end, section the cutlery divider into eight segments, each 7cm (2 3/4in) wide, and draw a vertical line down each section with the water-soluble marking pen, as shown in diagram 1.

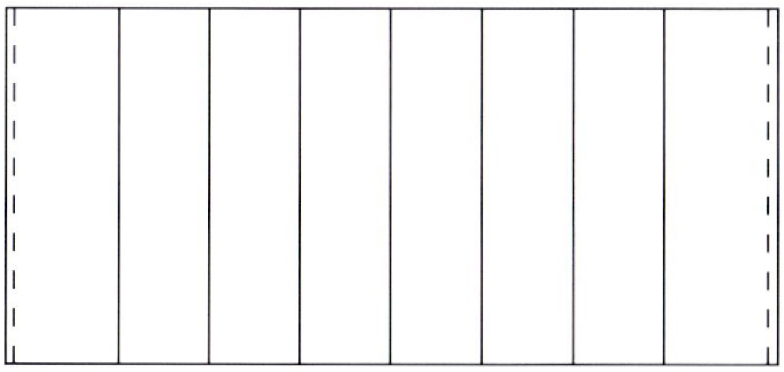

Diagram 1

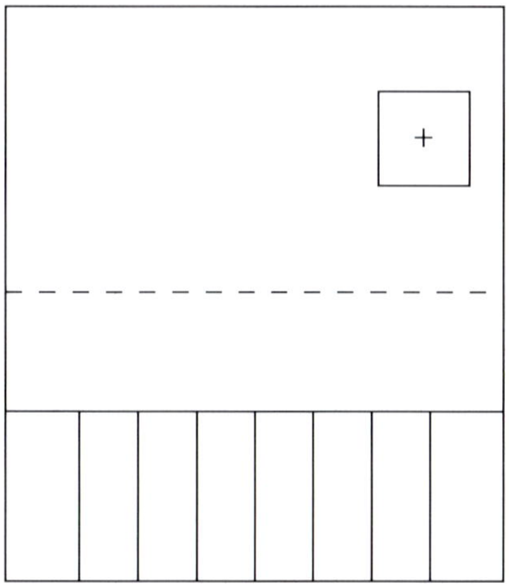

Diagram 2

Pin the cutlery divider to the lower edge of the main fabric and sew down the marked lines through both fabrics to form the cutlery pockets.

Cut the following pieces for the decorative work
One, 10cm (4in) square of plain fabric
Eight, 5cm (2in) squares patterned fabric
Two, 5cm (2in) squares in each of the two plain fabrics

Measure in 15cm (6in) from the top right corner, and 8cm (3in) in from the side edge, as a guide to placement of the decorative work. Mark the position with a water-soluble marking pen as shown in diagram 2.

Iron the fusible webbing to the back of the flower fabric for the appliqué. Cut out the flower shapes, remove the backing paper and press onto the 10cm (5in) plain fabric square.

Using the Custom Crafted Foot F and stitch 26, width 2, length 2, appliqué the flower edges. Iron fusible webbing to the back of this square.

To create the prairie points, fold the 12 squares in half and press. Bring each edge into the centre to create a smaller triangle and press well. Remove the paper backing from the appliquéd square and position over the placement mark.

Slide the raw edges of three prairie points under each side of the square. When positioning is correct, press the square in place.

Using a twin needle and the embroidery threads, select 31 and sew over the raw edges of the square.

To make the cutlery holder ties, fold the two 30cm x 6cm (12in x 2½in) strips in half and using the ¼in Seam Foot, stitch along the raw edges of the length of the strips. Turn the ties through to the right side and press.

For placement of the first tie, measure up 15cm (6in) from the lower edge and 29cm (11½in) from the side edge. Sew in position.

Pin the second tie to the side, 15cm (6in) up from the lower edge. This will be stitched into the side seam.

Iron Pellon to the lower half of the main fabric piece. With right sides together, fold the top half down to the lower edge and pin in place.

Using a straight stitch, sew around the edges leaving a small opening for turning.

Turn to the right side and hand-sew the opening closed. The finished size is 55cm x 30cm (21½in x 12in).

Bread Roll
HOLDER

Make this simple bread roll holder from coordinating fabric.

Requirements

- Shallow cane basket [approx. 25cm (10in) diameter]
- 35cm (14in) plain fabric
- 35cm (14in) patterned fabric
- 1.6/70 twin needle
- 2 embroidery threads in coordinating colours
- Tear-away stabiliser
- Fray Stoppa
- Sewing thread for construction
- 75cm (30in) narrow cord
- Water-soluble marking pen
- Eyelets – optional

Janome Accessories

- Blue-tipped needle

Method

From the plain fabric, cut one circle with a 35cm ($13^3/_4$in) diameter (or 10cm [4in] greater than the diameter of the purchased basket). From the patterned fabric, cut two circles with a 35cm ($13^3/_4$in) diameter.

Trace the bread roll holder template provided on the pattern sheet onto paper with the water-soluble marking pen and cut out. Fold the circles of fabric into quarters. Place the template on top of each folded circle and carefully draw around the scalloped edges.

Insert the twin needle into the sewing machine and thread with the two embroidery threads.

Set the machine to zig zag, width 4, length 0.3 With tear-away stabiliser placed behind the circles, sew around the drawn scallops. Sew each of the three circles in the same manner.

Apply Fray Stoppa to the edge of the scallop stitching, allow to dry, then carefully cut around the edge of the scallops.

Replace the twin needle with a blue-tipped needle and thread the machine with the construction sewing thread.

Following the template markings, draw the 12 eyelet positions on one of the patterned circle pieces and stitch the eyelets using stitch 21. If you do not have a machine with this stitch, purchased eyelets can be inserted following the manufacturer's instructions.

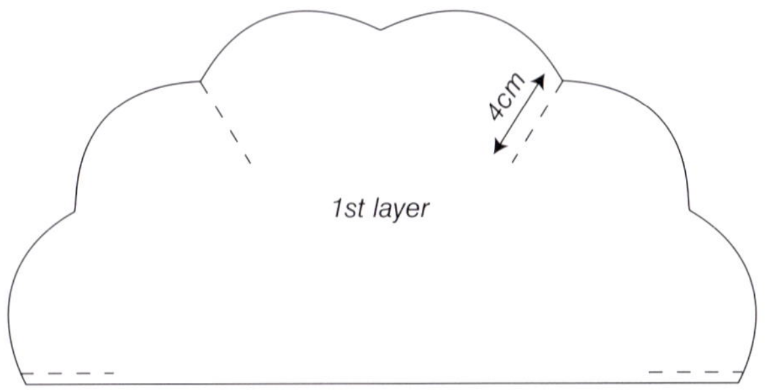

Diagram 1

With right sides facing up, place the plain fabric onto the patterned piece without the eyelets. Following the stitch markings on diagram 1 for the first layer, sew six lines, 4cm ($1^3/_8$in) long, through both fabric layers, from the outer edge, towards the centre.

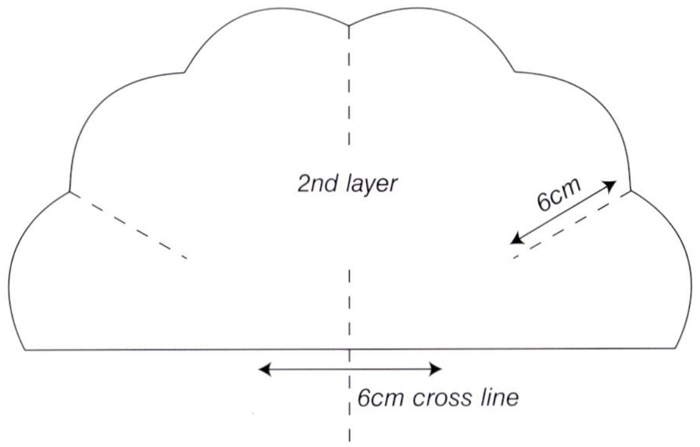

Diagram 2

Place the patterned piece with the eyelets onto the other two layers, right sides together.

Follow the stitch markings on diagram 2 for the second layer and sew six lines, 6cm ($2^1/_2$in) long, through the top two layers.

Mark a 6cm ($2^1/_2$in) cross in the centre of the top layer and stitch on the lines, through all three layers.

Catch the lower circle to the cane basket in three places with a darning needle. Thread the cord through the eyelets, pull up firmly and tie.

Buying a New Machine

So, you are off to buy a sewing machine, but where do you begin? There are so many brands and models, which one is the right one for you?

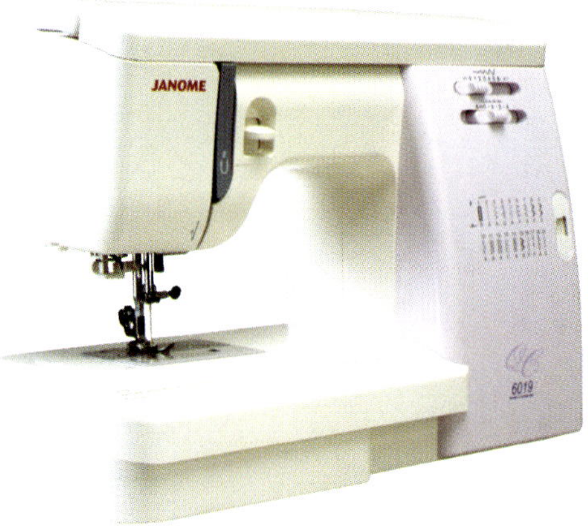

You can make the search much easier with some basic pre-planning. For instance, do you have a specific sewing interest or need? Have you decided how much you intend to spend on your sewing machine? This latter consideration is probably the best place to start, so set a budget.

If you are wanting to save money by sewing for your family, the stitch range of your ideal machine will include stitches suited to both knitted and woven fabrics or stretch and non-stretch fabrics, as well as for summer, winter and trans-seasonal weights of fabrics.

On the other hand, if you are planning mostly to purchase your garments and then individualise them with embellishments, you will require a sewing machine with those appropriate decorative or embroidery stitches.

If craft sewing or quilting are your hobbies then you will be attracted to a machine with those features that are beneficial to that type of sewing. Perhaps one of the five Quilter's Companion models from the extensive Janome range would be best. A further consideration could be the availability of optional accessories because these can extend the useful life of your machine by adding further dimensions to your sewing skills.

Also, remember that you are not the first or only person to be perplexed by making this decision, and if it is of some benefit, since the mid 1980s, over 60 per cent of ladies in Australia who have purchased a sewing machine have consistently chosen Janome. This is borne out by the import figures compiled by the Bureau of Statistics in Canberra.

By now you have a basic profile of the type of sewing machine which will be best suited to your requirements. Generally, sewing machines are available from both independent sewing machine specialist stores and larger department stores. The independent specialists can usually provide personal in store after sale warranty service and lessons. Most independents usually also have a more comprehensive range of machines on hand to demonstrate.

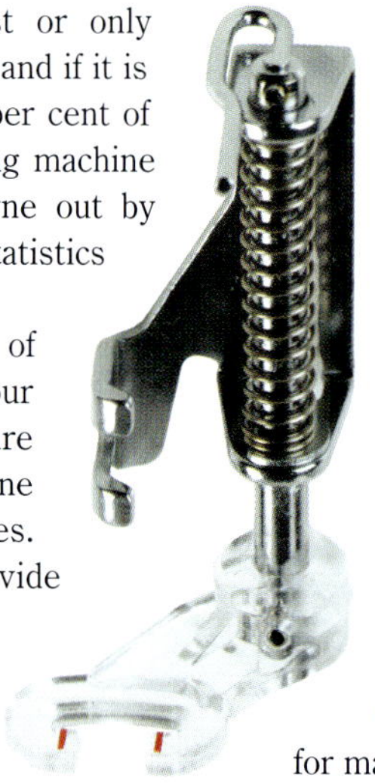

Discuss your particular sewing requirements with the in-store sewing consultant and don't be backward in participating in the demonstration. Take along some of your own fabric that you intend to use and ask if you can try the machine for yourself. You may find that you have extended your original profile, but you can be assured that you are actually defining the exact machine that is the ideal model for your needs. And in reality, this is the most practical way to find the best possible value you can achieve.

Eventually, you may return home with a small bundle of brochures. Read through these carefully and remember the manufacturers have identified all the important features of their product on their brochures.

Check through your list of requirements and compare them to the features that were pointed out to you during the demonstration in-store and those contained on the brochures. If you still have questions, return to the store and get the answers.

Also, ask yourself, does your choice of machine fit your budget? If not, most stores will let you lay-by. This is a good method of purchase especially if the machine has been reduced as part of a promotion or sale, otherwise wait and save up for it. It is a mistake to simply purchase a machine because the price suits your budget even though the features do not suit your sewing requirements.

Finally, ensure the place of purchase will be able to provide you with an acceptable level of after-sale service such as free lessons and a free service during the warranty period.

Following these suggestions will greatly reduce the risk of purchasing the wrong sewing machine and infinitely increase the probability that you will buy a sewing machine that you will continue to enjoy for many years to come.

Quilting Attachment Set

- Part Number 200100007

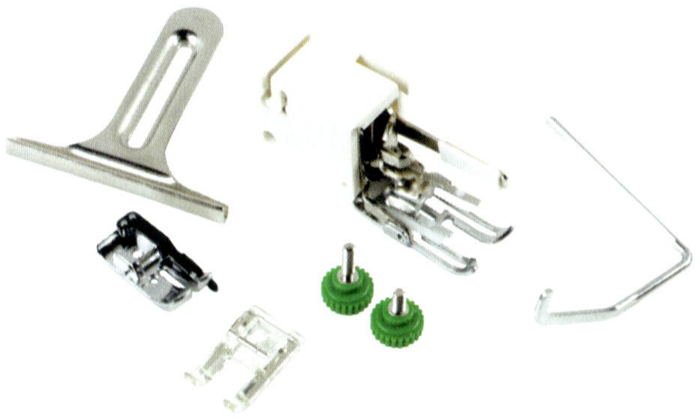

The following items are included in this set:

1/4in Seam Foot
A must for every patchworker. Using the black ridge at the side of the foot as a guide enables you to get a uniform 1/4in seam, every time.

Craft Foot
The craft foot or (F2 foot), is a satin stitch foot with a high ridge to allow high-density stitches to flow through without being dragged across the fabric. It has an open toe to allow better viewing when appliquéing and is highly recommended for any crafty person.

Walking Foot and Quilt Guide
A walking foot with its own feed dogs, allowing you to keep multi layers of fabric, lace fabric and even plaids together with little effort. The guide, built to fit in with the walking foot, makes quilting a delight.

Darning Foot
A darning foot with an open toe makes it easier to view your freehand creations as they happen. At present this handy item is only available in the Quilting Attachment set.

Cloth Guide
Ideal for any sewer, by attaching your cloth guide at the required width and guiding your fabric edge along it, you are certain to get the perfect edge on those curtains and other long straight edges required when quilting.

Rotary Cutting

Quilters have found that preparing, tracing around and cutting out templates is a time-consuming job. Rather than hand cut these shapes, multiple layers can be cut using a rotary cutter, ruler and cutting board.

When rotary cutting fabric it is important that you learn how to use your cutter correctly and safely.

Cutting Strips
The fabric must be correctly folded to ensure the cut strips are straight and accurate. Fold the fabric selvedge to selvedge first, lining up the straight of the grain as much as possible. This gives you four layers of fabric to cut through. Then fold the last fold to meet the first – this will give you eight layers.

Position the fabric on the cutting mat.

Align the folded edge with the horizontal grid lines on the mat. If you are right-handed the fabric should extend to the right, if you are left-handed it should extend to the left.

Align the acrylic ruler with the vertical grid lines of the mat. The first cut should remove the uneven edges of the fabric at the left side (for right-handed people). Place the ruler over the fabric so that the first cut will just remove all uneven edges.

With one smooth clean stroke, beginning before the fold, cut through to past the other fabric fold. Always cut away from yourself – never towards you.

Re-align the ruler to cut the first strip at the required width by aligning the grid on the ruler with the first cut in the fabric. If the strip is required to be 2in wide, then you should align the 2in grid line with the cut edge of the fabric. Cut along the edge of the ruler to create a 2in strip.

Always move the ruler for each subsequent strip – not the fabric. Unfold the first strip to ensure the cut edges are straight. If they are 'boomeranged' – a bend at each fold – then you may need to refold the fabric more carefully or align the ruler more accurately before cutting any more strips.

Cutting Squares
Once you have cut strips these can be crosscut into squares or rectangles. From a 2in wide strip it is possible to cut 2in squares – or any length rectangle.

Place the strips, either singly or a few aligned carefully side-by-side, onto the mat with the raw edges to the left (if you are right-handed). Align the ruler to the trimmed edge so the 2in grid line of the ruler is aligned to the cut edge of the fabric.

Safety First
Always keep fingers out of the way of the blade.
Apply firm pressure to the ruler when holding it in place to cut.
Apply even pressure to the cutter when cutting.
Close the blade cover after EVERY cut.
Replace the blade as soon as it becomes dull.
Blades should be oiled regularly.

35th Anniversary

Janome celebrates 35 years in Australia in 2004. Recognised as Australia's top-selling brand, Janome offers sewers a wide range of models – many at very affordable prices. On these pages we share a sampling of their current models – including new releases. To see these models and have a demonstration visit a Janome Sewing Machine dealer near you.

MEMORY CRAFT 10001

NEW RELEASE

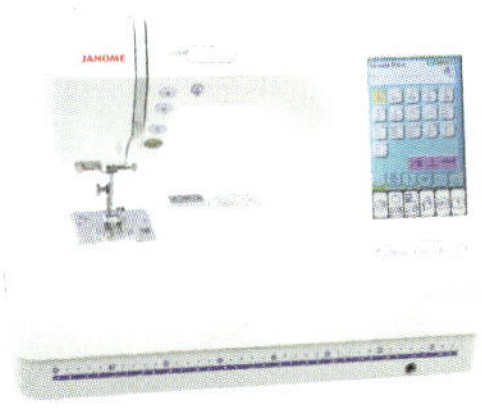

The sewing & embroidery machine that does it all!
- Over 250 utility & decorative stitches
- 11 one-step buttonholes
- 4 standard hoops, from the tiny Free Arm Hoop to the Giga Hoop
- Easy on-screen edits & layouts
- More ways to get designs in & out: internet, CD-ROMs, Memory Cards, PC design cards & ATA PC cards
- Patented telescoping carriage arm

MEMORY CRAFT 9500

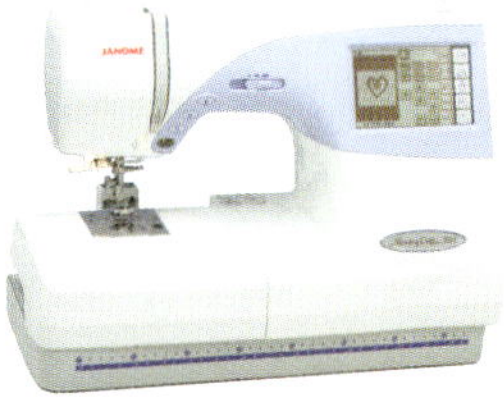

Sewing & embroidery with style
- 90 built-in embroidery designs incl. 10 large scale designs
- Standard & large hoops included
- Optional clothsetter for designs of virtually any size
- Easy, built-in design editing
- Huge selection of decorative stitches
- Download designs from the internet
- Update your machine with software

NEW RELEASE

MEMORY CRAFT 300E

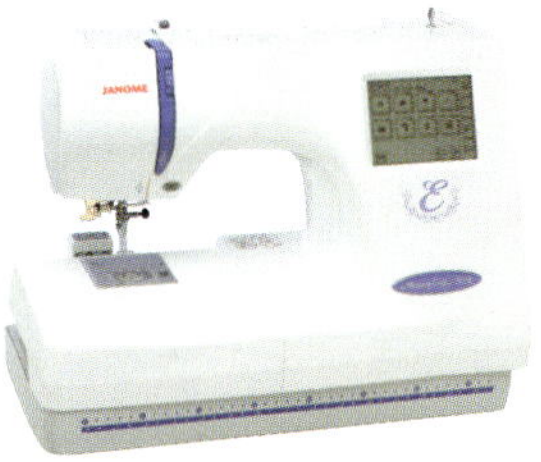

The embroidery-only specialist machine
- 90 built-in designs
- Bring in designs on PC design cards or ATA PC cards
- Can read up to 100 designs on an ATA PC card
- Standard & large hoops included
- Optional clothsetter for designs of virtually any size
- Update your machine through software

NEW RELEASE

MEMORY CRAFT 6500P

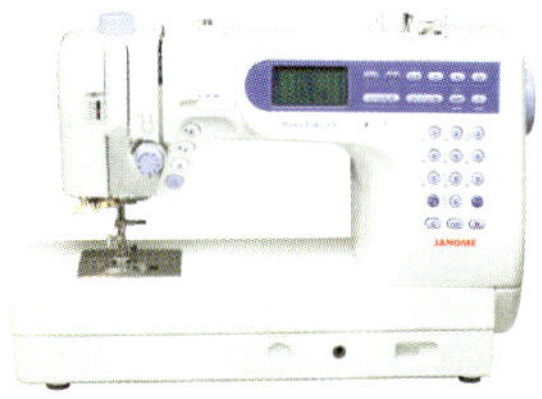

Perfect for quilters or home sewers
- Huge work space makes sewing a breeze
- Incredibly fast sewing 1000 s.p.m. for straight stitch (700 s.p.m. for zigzag stitches)
- Automatic thread cutter
- 128 built-in stitches + 7 buttonholes+ monograms
- Large extension table included
- Knee lifter for your convenience
- Quick pattern reference chart
- Independent motor for bobbin winding

NEW RELEASE

MEMORY CRAFT 4800

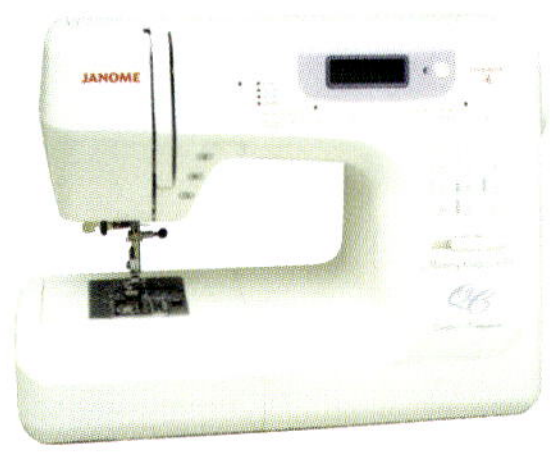

QUILTERS COMPANION
- Fully computerised
- Soft touch pattern selection
- Visual sewing screen
- 233 editable stitches including two styles of lettering
- 5 buttonhole styles
- Store key to recall patterns
- Speed setting lever

MEMORY CRAFT 3500

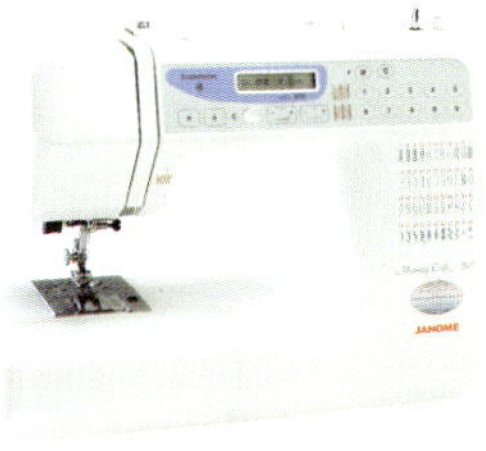

- Fully computerised
- 4 automatic buttonholes
- LCD message screen indicates stitch, foot and thread tension
- 46 practical & decorative stitches
- Halogen lamp for brighter sewing area
- Built-in needle threader
- Strong needle penetration power
- Simple to use

QUILTER'S COMPANION 6260

Experience the speed & precision of this computerised machine

- 60 stitches including six types of buttonholes
- Bright LED screen
- Automatic upper thread tension
- Max. 7mm stitch width control
- Includes Quilting Attachment Kit & hard cover

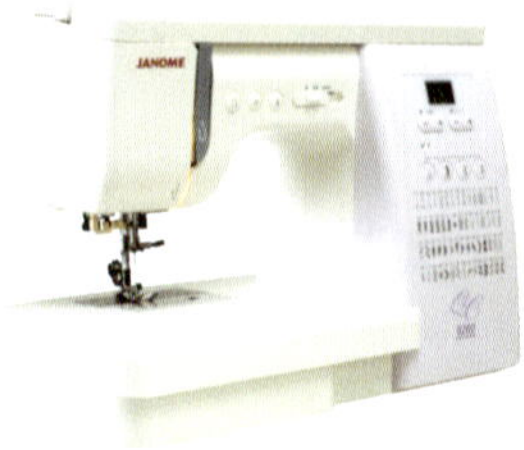

JANOME 419S

- 19 Stitches
- Adjustable foot pressure
- One-step buttonhole
- Auto-declutch bobbin winder
- Stitch length & width adjustment lever
- Convenient one-hand thread cutter
- Built-in needle threader
- Quick foot conversion
- Sewing on heavy weight fabrics
- Extension table
- Drop feed lever

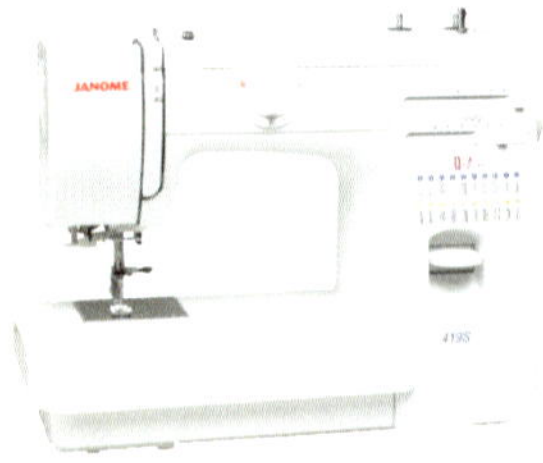

NEW RELEASE

QUILTER'S COMPANION 6125

Automatic functions & features that quilters love

- 25 stitches & one-step buttonhole
- Max. 6.5mm stitch width control
- Automatic needle threader
- Includes Quilting Attachment Kit & hard cover
- LCD guide screen

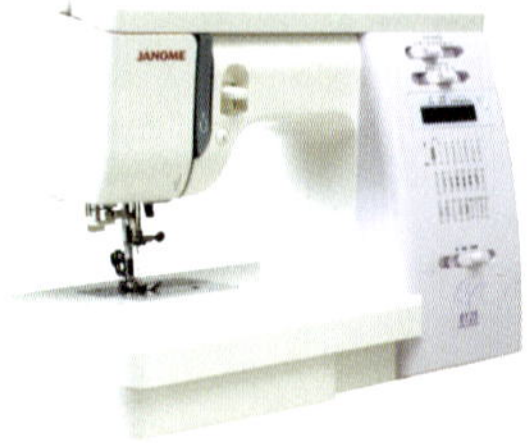

JANOME 415

- Auto declutch bobbin winder
- Built-in needle threader
- Built-in storage compartment
- 15 built-in stitches
- Four-step auto buttonhole
- Carry handle
- Convertible free arm
- Decorative stitches
- Drop feed
- Extra high presser foot
- Hidden tension dial
- Length & width control
- Needle plate guide lines
- One hand thread cutter
- Protective hard cover
- Quick rule on extension table
- Sews extra heavy weight fabrics
- Snap-on feet

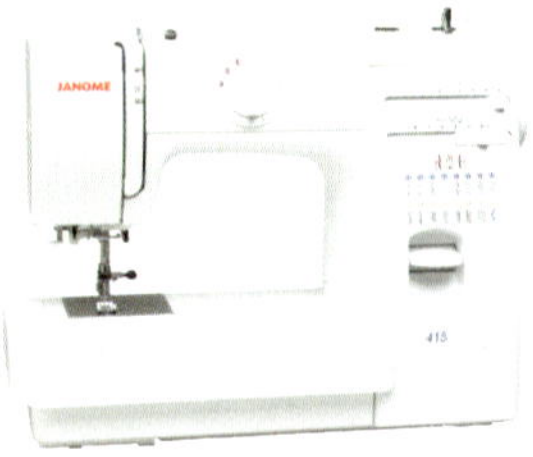

NEW RELEASE

QUILTER'S COMPANION 6019

The most affordable quilting machine

- 19 stitches & one step buttonhole
- Stitch indication window
- Automatic needle threader
- Includes Quilting Attachment Kit & hard cover

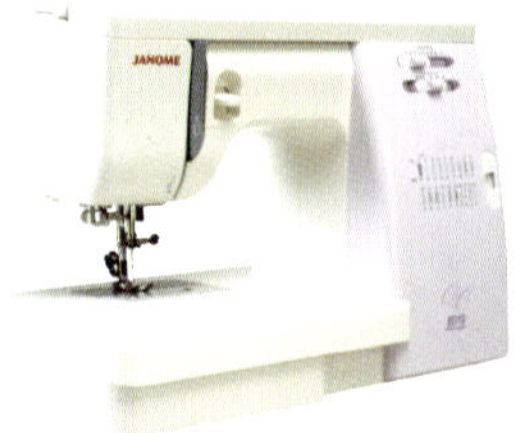

MY LOCK 644D

- 2, 3 or 4 thread overlocking
- Differential feed
- Easy rolled hem changeover
- Smooth fabric feed
- Plus much more!

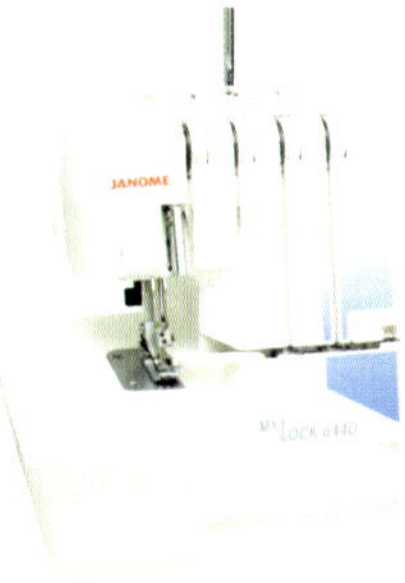

JANOME 4618 QC

QUILTERS COMPANION

- One-step buttonhole
- Jam proof top loading bobbin
- Quick foot conversion
- Convenient top storage exclusive to Janome

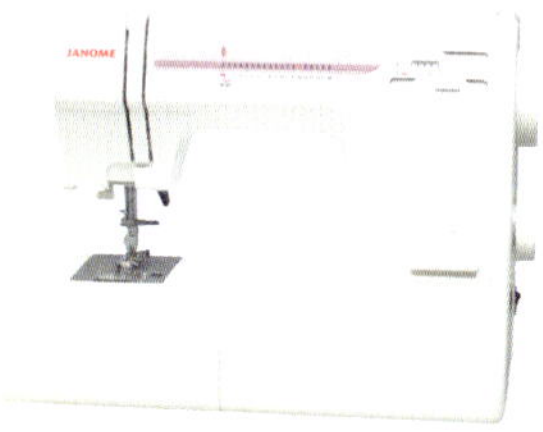

MY LOCK 204D

- 3/4 thread overlocker
- Adjustable differential feed
- Adjustable stitch length
- Colour coded threading
- Easy rolled hem change over
- Smooth vibration-free performance

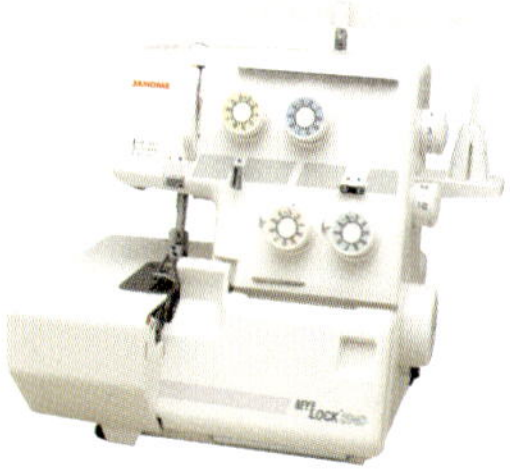

Quilter's Companion Models Stitch Comparison

Stitch Symbol	4800QC	6260QC	6125QC	6019QC	Stitch Symbol	4800QC	6260QC	6125QC	6019QC
	45	32	15	–		65	30	20	14
	46	31	10	8		36	–	17	11
	51	33	–	–		71	24	21	15
	47	36	11	9		61	42	–	–
	53	37	–	–		93	54	–	–
	50	38	14	–		85	52	–	–
	52	39	12	–		70	53	–	–
	30	7	23	17		80	59	–	–
	26	25	22	16		67	56	–	–
	31	29	–	–		76	50	–	–
	44	46	–	–		7	11	–	–
	40	44	–	–		15	14	4	4
						21	22	–	–

Selecting the best needle for your project

Blue Tip

The premium Janome needle.

Specially designed for Janome embroidery machines and general sewing on most fabric types.

Part Number	Size	Number Per Pack
990311000	#11	5

Ballpoint

Preferred for stretch and knit fabrics.

Specially designed with a rounded tip that separates fabric fibres to prevent skipping stitches or damaging fabric. Used for fabrics such as cotton knits, tricot, jersey knits and swimsuit fabric.

Part Number	Size	Number Per Pack
990211000	#11	5
990214000	#14	5
990200000	Ass.	1/#9 1/#11 3/#14

Denim

Preferred for heavyweight fabrics.

A special wedge-shaped tip produces optimum results on medium to heavyweight denim.

Part Number	Size	Number Per Pack
990416000	#16	5

Red tip, size 14

Preferred for embroidery on heavyweight fabrics.

It has extra strength and durability for denser embroidery and thicker fabric. Equipped with a large eye, it is ideal for tricky threads (like metallic threads) and helps to prevent thread breakages.

Part number	Size	Number Per Pack
990314000	#14	5

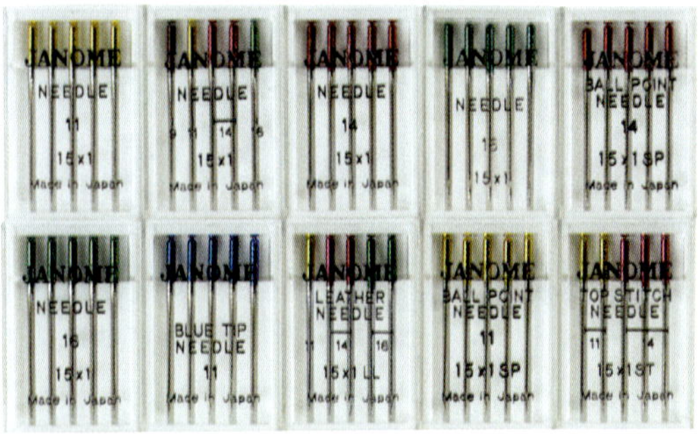

Topstitch

Ideal for decorative sewing.

Specially designed to accommodate heavier threads for decorative stitching. Choose the needle size based on the weight of the fabric.

Part Number	Size	Number Per Pack
990500000	Ass.	2/#11, 3/#14

Universal

Preferred for woven fabric.

For general-purpose sewing on woven fabrics. Use for fabrics such as silks, cottons, linens and crepes. Choose the needle size based on the weight of the fabric.

Part Number	Size	Number Per Pack
990109000	# 9	5
990111000	#11	5
990112000	#12	5
990114000	#14	5
990116000	#16	5
990100000	Asst.	1 x #9, 1 x #11 2 x #14, 1 x #16

Leather

Preferred for genuine and faux leather.

Specially designed needlepoint provides smooth, even stitching. Use for leather and suede fabrics.

Part Number	Size	Number Per Pack
990600000	Ass.	1/#11, 2/#14, 2/#16

ACKNOWLEDGEMENTS

Many people have assisted in the creation of this book,
by sharing their time, products or expertise and we thank them all.

Bill Day, Dayview Textiles
Stan Woodrow, Taree Sewing Centre
Marilyn Davies, Janome Western Australia
Margaret Langford, Janome Victoria
Yetty Barrett, Janome Victoria
Irene Cowie, Janome New South Wales
Isabella Ceravolo, Janome New South Wales
Maryann Sanders, Janome New South Wales
Trish Lang, Janome Sewing Centre Bunbury and Rockingham
Judith Hardaker, Sewrite Sewing Centre
Judy Dunn, Janome Bankstown
Karleen Pratt, Janome Wollongong
Ismay Frith, Janome Sewing Advisor

General prints, patterns and fabrics have been used in the projects, and substitutions will also provide satisfactory results. In the case of the Bedroom and Baby's Room projects fabrics have been supplied by Dayview Textiles, the Australian distributor for RJR Fabrics. The Sunshine Acres range was used in the Baby's Room. Willow Mews range was used in the Bedroom. Dayview Textiles can be contacted on (02) 9600 8811, fax (02) 9600 8811, email dayview@ozemail.com.au

Each project was created by talented Janome people from around Australia – they are:

Bedroom

Cushions by Ismay Frith
Flying Down the Borders quilt, valance and curtains by Isabella Ceravolo

Baby's Room

Irish Hearts Quilt, Irish Heart Wallhanging, Towel and Washer, Curtain Tie Backs and Bed Linen by Irene Cowie
Basket by Judith Hardaker
Butterflies by Judy Dunn
Lacey Lucy by Judith Hardaker

Sitting Room

Cushion by Trish Lang
Lampshade and Footsool by Marilyn Davies
Freehand Embroidered Landscape by Karleen Pratt

Outdoor Setting

Serviettes and Serviette Rings by Margaret Langford
Chef's Hat, Apron and Oven Mitt by Yetty Barrett
Cutlery Roll, Placemats, Director's Chairs and Bread Roll Holder by Margaret Langford

Janome Head Office Telephone (03) 9584 7622, www.janome.com.au